WOODEN BOWLS

from the SCROLL SAW

WOODEN BOWLS

from the SCROLL SAW

28 Useful & Surprisingly Easy-to-Make Projects

Carole Rothman

FOX CHAPEL
PUBLISHING

About the Author

Carole Rothman, a psychologist and retired college professor, has been a craftsperson for most of her life. Her goal has long been to give her work a distinctive look by integrating concepts from many crafts, applying them in unexpected ways, then sharing her discoveries with others. As a cake decorator, for example, her innovative designs won her national recognition and the opportunity to write for and teach others. Currently, she is applying her talents to the scroll saw with the same creative and educational goals in mind.

A collapsible wooden basket, purchased several years ago at a crafts fair, was the impetus for Carole to learn the scroll saw. After mastering basic skills by cutting scores of boxes, puzzles, and baskets, she began applying concepts from needlework and cake decorating to her scroll saw work. Her projects, for which she has won awards and recognition, are always interesting and challenging. Because she often uses the cut-offs from one creation as the starting point for the next, she rarely lacks the raw materials needed for her projects. On the other hand, she is chronically short of storage room.

Acknowledgements

Thanks to the following people, without whom I could not have written this book: My best friend and partner, Joe Ilardo, for his invaluable support, and for the many hours he spent patiently checking my work. The staff at Fox Chapel, who have guided me along the way, especially: my editor, Kerri Landis; Acquisition Editor, Peg Couch; and Shannon Flowers, Editorial Manager of *Scroll Saw Woodworking & Crafts* magazine. My sons, Dan and Jon Rothman, and Janine Tesbir, whose confidence in my abilities has been a constant comfort.

ISBN 978-1-56523-433-8

Library of Congress Cataloging-in-Publication Data

Rothman, Carole.

Wooden bowls from the scroll saw : 28 useful & surprisingly easy-to-make projects / Carole Rothman.

   p. ; cm.

Includes index.

ISBN: 978-1-56523-433-8

1. Jig saws. 2. Woodwork--Patterns. 3. Bowls (Tableware) I. Title.

TT186.R73 2009
745.51'3--dc22

             2009022923

To learn more about the other great books from Fox Chapel Publishing, or to find a retailer near you, call toll-free 800-457-9112 or visit us at *www.FoxChapelPublishing.com*.

Note to Authors: We are always looking for talented authors to write new books. Please send a brief letter describing your idea to Acquisition Editor, 1970 Broad Street, East Petersburg, PA 17520.

Printed in China
Fourth printing

Contents

Introduction: About This Book - 6

Chapter One: Getting Started - 8

Chapter Two: Basic Stacked Bowls - 20
    Basic Bowl: A Step-by-Step Guide - 22
    Eight-Petal Bowl - 30
    Rounded-Square Bowl - 52
    Wavy Bowl - 34
    Scrolled-Top Bowl - 36

Chapter Three: Laminated Wood Bowls - - - - - - - - - - - - - - - - - - 40
    Double-Swag Bowl: A Step-by-Step Guide - - - - - - - - - - - - - 42
    Basket-Weave Bowl - 46
    Plaid Bowl - 49
    Gingham Bowl - 52
    Windowpane Bowl - 54
    Triple-Swirl Bowl - 57

Chapter Four: Multiple-Angle Bowls - - - - - - - - - - - - - - - - - - - 60
    Crisscross Bowl: A Step-by-Step Guide - - - - - - - - - - - - - - - 62
    Flared Five-Lobed Bowl - 68
    Ripple-Edged Round Bowl - 70
    Four-Petal Curved Bowl - 74
    Heart-Shaped Bowl - 76

Chapter Five: Thin Wood Bowls - 78
    Eight-Segment Bowl: A Step-by-Step Guide - - - - - - - - - - - 80
    Multi-Colored Twenty Segment Bowl - - - - - - - - - - - - - - - 86
    Seven-Lobe Ripple-Edged Bowl - - - - - - - - - - - - - - - - - - - 90
    Oval Bowl - 92
    Center Lamination Bowl - 94
    Five-Petal Bowl - 96

Chapter Six: Thinking Outside the Bowl - - - - - - - - - - - - - - - - - 98
    Double-Swirl Vase: A Step-by-Step Guide - - - - - - - - - - - - 100
    Ginger Jar - 107
    Multi-Colored Jar - 113
    Footed Candy Dish - 118
    Rounded Vase with Laminated Rings - - - - - - - - - - - - - - - 122
    Ripple-Edged Vase - 126

Appendix: Creating Patterns - 132

Index - 135

Introduction: About This Book

I've always had mixed feelings about lathe-turned bowls: loved the bowls, hated the waste. When I learned that angled cuts on the scroll saw could produce beautiful bowls from flat pieces of wood, I had to give it a try. My first bowl, a simple one created from plans I drew up on graph paper, convinced me that a lot more could be done.

Flying somewhat blind, I tried different shapes and angles, different woods and laminations. Not everything worked, but as I cut and glued and sanded, I gradually learned how to create and reproduce the effects I wanted. The projects in this book are the results.

The book starts where I began, with a simple aspen bowl. Each chapter introduces a different aspect of bowl making, and many projects use techniques introduced earlier in the book. Regardless of experience or skill level, you're likely to find projects that suit your needs and preferences. And when you're ready to move beyond this book, the last chapter will give you the information you need to design your own beautiful bowls.

Happy scrolling!
Carole

Round Bowls

Basic Bowl and alternate, page 22

Scrolled-Top Bowl, page 36

Double-Swag Bowl, page 42

Basket-Weave Bowl and alternate, page 46

Plaid Bowl, page 49

Gingham Bowl and alternate, page 52

Triple-Swirl Bowl and alternate, page 57

Eight-Segment Bowl and alternate, page 80

Multi-Colored Twenty Segment Bowl, page 86

Footed Candy Dish, page 118

Jars

Ginger Jar, page 107

Multi-Colored Jar, page 113

Petal Bowls

Eight-Petal Bowl, page 30

Four-Petal Curved Bowl, page 74

Five-Petal Bowl, page 96

Wavy-Edged Bowls

Wavy Bowl, page 34

Flared Five-Lobed Bowl, page 68

Ripple-Edged Round Bowl, page 70

Seven-Lobe Ripple-Edged Bowl, page 90

Rectangular Bowls

Rounded-Square Bowl, page 32

Windowpane Bowl, page 54

Crisscross Bowl, page 62

Center Lamination Bowl, page 94

Other Bowls

Heart-Shaped Bowl, page 76

Oval Bowl, page 92

Vases

Double-Swirl Vase, page 100

Rounded Vase with Laminated Rings, page 122

Ripple-Edged Vase, page 126

1

Getting Started

Making bowls with the scroll saw is fun, creative, and rewarding. Making a three-dimensional object from a flat piece of wood is quite amazing, not to mention economical. It's also a perfect way to use up wood you have on hand. This chapter introduces you to the materials, tools, and techniques you'll need to scroll your bowl.

Bowl making consists of six steps, which I will describe in this chapter: choosing the wood, cutting the rings, drilling entry holes, gluing, sanding, and applying the finish.

Cutting the bowls in this book requires tilting your scroll saw table. The angle is determined by width of the rings and the thickness of the stock used.

Attention to grain and color helps ensure an attractive bowl.

Choosing the Wood

Most of the projects in this book are made from pieces of ¾" (19mm)-thick stock with a maximum width of 8" (203mm). These pieces are cut into concentric rings which, when stacked, form bowls. The rings must be cut accurately to line up properly. For this to occur, the wood used must be soft enough to be cut at a steep angle. Woods that are very hard or dense can deflect the blade and distort the rings. They are frustrating to use as the main bowl stock. However, even these woods may be usable as strips for lamination or for bowls that specifically call for thinner stock. Since wood characteristics can vary from board to board, try a test cut on any wood that seems marginal.

Selecting wood species

Most commonly available woods are appropriate for use as the primary wood, including aspen, poplar, mahogany, maple, cherry, walnut, cedar, and oak. Most of these woods can also be used for laminations. Be sure to use wood that is thoroughly dry, kiln dried if possible, to minimize the likelihood of delamination.

Aspen

Although seldom recommended because of its softness, aspen is inexpensive, easy to cut and shape, and when sanded well and shellacked, looks like ivory or porcelain. Its lack of pronounced grain is desirable for certain types of projects, but its softness makes it a poor choice for lamination unless the contrasting wood is also soft.

Poplar

Inexpensive and easy to cut, poplar is attractive when clear and light-colored. Choose carefully to avoid pieces with large brownish green patches.

Cedar

Fragrant, soft, and easy to cut, cedar is a good choice for bowls. It is, however, prone to fracture along small fault lines and needs gentle handling. Small breaks, should they occur, can usually be glued up so they won't show.

> **Choose wood carefully**
> Examine boards before you buy them. Wood that is warped or contains defects is usually the same price as straight pieces with attractive grain.

Mahogany

Mahogany is easy to cut, sand, and finish. The fact that its grain is not pronounced makes it a good choice for projects such as a vase, which require more than one piece of the same type of wood. There are many varieties, varying in cost, but even the less expensive ones make attractive bowls.

Maple

Readily available, maple is a good choice for a light-colored bowl, or to highlight darker laminations. Color varies; choose carefully to get the effect you want.

Cherry

Always elegant, cherry finishes beautifully and is often used for bowls. However, to prevent burn marks, the wood should be covered with tape before cutting to provide lubrication for the blade.

Walnut

Easy to cut and finish, walnut provides good contrast with lighter colored woods such as cherry and maple. If its somewhat higher cost is a deterrent, use it as an accent in laminations.

Oak

Oak is appropriate both as a stand-alone wood and as a color contrast for lamination. Pieces with straight grain are more attractive than those with wild grain patterns.

Other woods

Don't be afraid to try unfamiliar or exotic woods. Cutting a test ring is the best way to determine whether a wood is usable. I've had success with teak, lacewood, and hickory in standard thicknesses, and with zebrawood as thinner stock.

Choosing wood for lamination

In choosing wood for lamination, there are three factors to keep in mind.

Color contrast

Color contrast can be subtle, such as a poplar and cedar combination, or dramatic, such as a pairing of walnut and maple. To preview what the finished combination will look like, apply mineral spirits to each piece.

Hardness

Woods that are similar in hardness, such as cherry and maple, will be easier to sand smooth when glued together. Woods that are dissimilar, such as cherry and mahogany, have to be sanded more carefully to avoid removing too much of the softer wood.

Color bleeding

Padauk, an extremely colorful orange wood, can discolor adjacent pieces of lighter-colored or more porous woods. If you use a combination such as padauk and cedar, be vigilant about vacuuming up sanding dust, and apply your finish sparingly.

Recycled Wood

Many of the bowls in this book were cut from recycled wood. I discovered large boards of mahogany and teak, covered with a layer of varnish, in an old storage shed. I retrieved maple from my sons' baby dresser. Another woodworker's scraps provided cherry for lamination. I've also gone "dumpster diving" at a local staircase factory. Be creative with your sources. You'll benefit, and so will the environment.

Cutting the Rings

All projects in this book are based on a series of rings cut at steep angles. Beginning projects use patterns to guide all cuts. Later projects use patterns that provide an outline and first ring only; once cut, each ring serves as the pattern for the next. This method requires more precise cutting, but produces a better alignment. When the bowl shape is based on a circle and the wood is not too dark, the pattern can be drawn directly on the wood using a compass to make one or a series of rings. This allows for maximum flexibility in sizing a project, and maximum visibility for centering rings on a laminated bank. All patterns should be attached with repositionable adhesive for best results.

Regardless of the method used, the cutting procedures are the same, and require good quality aggressive blades. After trying many brands and blade types, I found Flying Dutchman reverse and ultra reverse blades to be consistently excellent. I use #9 for cutting all bowl blanks; it's large enough to handle thick stock but still takes a fairly small entry hole. Tension must be tight to minimize distortion while cutting thick wood at a steep angle. Where size of entry holes is not a factor, as when cutting wood for laminations or inserts, you can use any blade you prefer, such as a #12 for thick wood and a #3 or #5 for thinner stock.

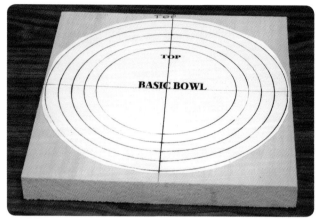

Beginning projects, such as the basic bowl, include a pattern for each ring.

More advanced projects will have a pattern for the first ring only. Each ring will then be used to create the next one.

The useful awl

In this book, the awl is used for several important purposes. The first is to center patterns on the blank, which is done by inserting the point of the awl through the center of the pattern and placing it at the intersection of the guidelines. The second purpose is to create an indentation to keep the drill bit from wandering when drilling an entry hole with an angle guide. Be sure to keep your awl handy while progressing through the projects.

Marking the bowl

Pencil marks of various types are made on the bowl blank in the course of making the bowl, and the type of pencil lead used can make a difference. Hard lead pencils, such as 2H or 4H, make it easy to draw thin lines, which permit more precise cutting and alignment than thicker ones. In addition, hard lead discharges fewer graphite particles than soft lead. This is desirable because graphite particles can penetrate the fibers of soft woods, such as aspen, too deeply to be sanded out. For these reasons, it makes sense to use a hard lead pencil whenever possible, and to erase all unneeded pencil marks before gluing up and sanding. On dark woods like walnut or teak, a white pencil can make markings easier to see.

Blade tensioning

1. If blade slippage occurs when using higher tension, the blade ends can be lightly sanded to remove any residual oil. Clamping screws can also be sanded or filed to remove any oil, dirt, or burrs that may be contributing to the problem.

2. The blade holders on some scroll saws require considerable finger strength to tighten sufficiently to prevent slippage. This problem can be solved with an easy-to-make tightener that slips over the knob. To make this simple device, trace the outline of your scroll saw's blade-holder knob on a small block of wood, drill out the center, and cut along the outline. Be careful not to over tighten to avoid stripping threads or breaking the clamp.

This shop-made device makes it easy to tighten blade holders.

Table tilt and cutting direction

There are two factors to consider when cutting at an angle: whether the saw table is tilted left or right side down, and whether the cut is in a clockwise or counterclockwise direction. Unless indicated otherwise, all angled cuts for projects in this book are made with the saw table tilted left side down. Nearly all cuts are made in a clockwise direction. When the instructions say to cut in a clockwise direction, this means that you are turning the wood in a counterclockwise direction as you cut. In other words, the *blade* appears to be moving clockwise because the *wood* is moving counterclockwise. A circle cut in this manner, with the saw table tilted left side down, is wider at the top than at the bottom. Those few situations where counterclockwise cutting is needed are indicated clearly in boldface.

All about angles

For every combination of wood thickness and ring width, there is a cutting angle that will result in a near-perfect alignment when concentric rings are cut and stacked. The chart below gives the cutting angles for three different ring widths, using ½" or ¾" (13mm or 19mm) stock, which will result in a near-perfect alignment. This angle is used to create a straight-sided bowl from a single piece of wood. Use of multiple angles to produce curved sides and other effects is introduced in Chapter Four (page 60).

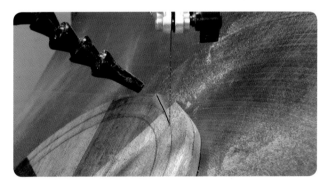

Cutting a ring in a clockwise direction means that the wood is moving counterclockwise. The cut will be wider on the upper face than on the lower one.

Cutting angles for straight-sided bowls

Wood thickness	Ring width	Cutting angle
½" (13mm) stock	½" (13mm)	45°
½" (13mm) stock	⅜" (10mm)	38°
½" (13mm) stock	¼" (6mm)	28°
¾" (19mm) stock	½" (13mm)	34°
¾" (19mm) stock	⅜" (10mm)	28°
¾" (19mm) stock	¼" (6mm)	20°

Changing project size

If you wish to change the size of a project in this book by reducing or enlarging the pattern, you must either redraw the rings to their original width or change the cutting angle. If you want to change wood thickness, you must also re-compute the cutting angle. Refer to the chart on page 134.

Drilling Entry Holes

Once the outer profile of the first ring is cut, an entry hole is needed to cut the inner circle of that ring. The angle of this hole is usually the same as the one used for the outer cut, and will be clearly specified in the instructions. You can use either a drill press with a tilting table or a shop-made drilling angle guide to obtain the correct angle. If rings are less than 3/8" (10mm) wide, try to avoid back-to-back entry holes. Always use the smallest drill bit that allows your blade to pass through. I use a #54 bit, which is slightly smaller than 1/16" (2mm), for the #9 blade.

Drill starter holes using the smallest bit that will accommodate your blade. The smaller the hole, the easier the sanding will be later on.

Making and using an angle guide

Cut a scrap of ¾" (19mm)-thick hardwood into a rectangle measuring about 2" x 1½" (51mm x 38mm). Cut one side to the desired angle and mark this angle on top for future reference. To use the guide, mark the entry hole on the pattern with an awl. Place the edge of the guide at the hole, angled edge toward the center of the bowl blank. Place the drill bit along the guide and drill through the blank. If the bit is too short to go all of the way through with the guide in place, slide the guide out of the way to complete the hole.

Having an assortment of angle guides on hand makes it easy to drill a hole at the proper angle.

Gluing

After the rings are cut, they must be aligned and glued up. I use a two-stage gluing process in which the rings are glued up first without the bottom piece. The bottom piece is glued on only after the inside faces of the rings are shaped and sanded smooth. Once the bottom is glued on, further sanding of the inside bottom edge is not possible. At each stage, firm clamping is essential. Although conventional clamps or heavy books can be used, a bowl press helps keep the alignment while exerting strong, even pressure.

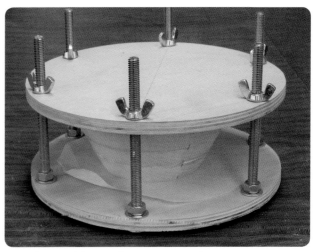

Evenly distributed downward pressure is essential for gluing up rings properly.

Which glue to use?

Choosing the correct glue is extremely important when gluing up bowls, because glue creep due to seasonal changes can create unattractive ridges.

Regular PVA

Regular white polyvinyl acetate (PVA) glue is not recommended because its pliability after drying may result in rings moving slightly out of alignment.

Weldbond and Weldwood are both appropriate adhesives, as is Titebond II or III.

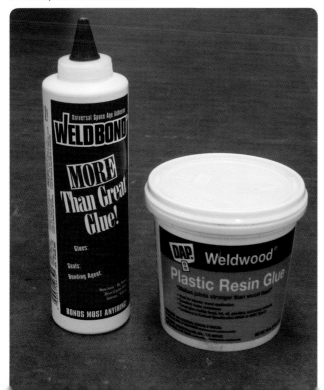

Advanced PVA

More advanced PVA glues such as Titebond II and III are stronger and more water resistant, and are better choices. I was concerned about the dark color of Titebond III, but found that even with aspen, the dark color was not a problem provided the rings fit tightly against each other.

Catalyzed PVA

Weldbond, a catalyzed PVA glue, was used for the projects in this book because I like its quick tack, which keeps rings from slipping out of alignment during glue-up. This quality makes it an ideal choice for laminations that are difficult to clamp without slippage. It is non-toxic and dries hard and clear. However, the glue between rings tends to soften temporarily from the heat generated by sanding. This softened glue can re-deposit itself on the bowl surface and must be sanded off.

Urea-formaldehyde

I also tried Weldwood, a urea-formaldehyde glue, which dries hard, is heat resistant, and is not subject to ring creep. Weldwood comes in powder form and must be mixed fresh for each use. It cleans up with water, and is easy to apply. However, the powder is carcinogenic, making a dust mask mandatory, and the glue requires a long clamping time (12 to 24 hours under normal shop conditions).

Making a bowl press

A shop-made bowl press, with optional spacers, is invaluable to prevent slippage as you glue up your bowl rings. Though you can use other methods of clamping, a bowl press is the easiest and quickest way to exert an even amount of pressure across the bowl being clamped.

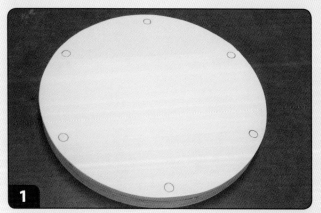

1

Cutting the plywood. Stack the plywood and attach the pieces to each other with double-sided tape. Center pattern and cut out the perimeter with a scroll saw or band saw. Do not separate the circles.

2

Drilling the holes. Drill through both pieces of wood with a ⅜" (10mm) bit at the six places indicated on the pattern. Make an alignment mark on the edge of the pieces.

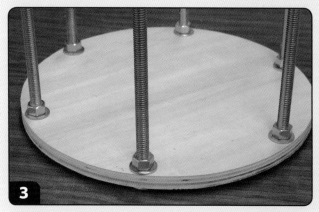

3

Completing the press. Separate the pieces. Push a carriage bolt through each hole on one of the pieces. This will be the base of your press. Place a washer and nut on top of the base and tighten the nuts evenly all around until the bolts are drawn in tightly. Enlarge the holes slightly on the second piece with a circular file or spindle sander until it fits easily over the bolts.

4

Using the press. To use the press, place a piece of wax paper on the base, place the glued-up rings on the wax paper, and place another piece of wax paper on top of the rings. Slide the top plate over the bolts. Tighten the wing nuts alternately until evenly tight. Do not over-tighten or the rings can distort.

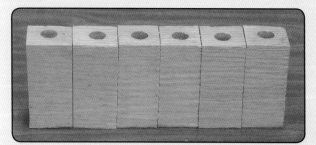

Spacers are useful accessories if you are gluing up just a few rings or a low bowl. They slide over the bolts after the top is in place, and allow you to tighten the press quickly. Use a hard wood that is at least 1" (25mm) thick, and as wide as the height you need.

Stand the wood on its side and mark six drilling holes spaced about 1½" (38mm) apart. Drill through the wood with a ⁷⁄₁₆" (11mm) bit. Set the wood on its face and cut between the holes, forming six blocks. The spacers in the photo are about 1¼" x 1¼" x 2½" (32mm x 32mm x 64mm).

Materials and Tools

Materials

* (2) 10" (254mm) squares of ½" (13mm) plywood
* (6) ⅜" (10mm) x 6" (152mm) carriage bolts, non-galvanized
* (6) Nuts to fit the carriage bolts, non-galvanized
* (6) Washers to fit the carriage bolts, non-galvanized
* (6) Wing nuts to fit the carriage bolts, non-galvanized
* Double-sided tape
* 1¼" (32mm) x 2½" (64mm) x 9" (229mm) piece of hardwood for spacers (optional)

Tools

* ⅜" (10mm) (press) drill bit
* ⁷⁄₁₆" (11mm) (spacers) drill bit
* Wrench to tighten nuts

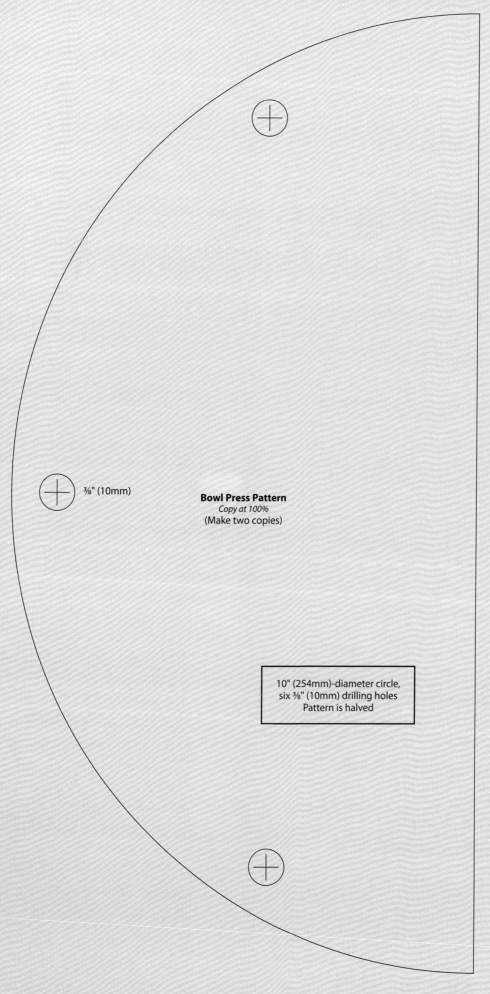

⅜" (10mm)

Bowl Press Pattern
Copy at 100%
(Make two copies)

10" (254mm)-diameter circle,
six ⅜" (10mm) drilling holes
Pattern is halved

Sanding

Sanding is the basic technique used to transform a raggedy set of rings into a work of art. As with intarsia, it is used for shaping as well as smoothing the surface. Inner and outer surfaces are shaped with more aggressive grits, such as 60 or 80, depending on the hardness of the wood. Once shaped, sanding is done with progressively finer grits until the desired smoothness is reached. Depending on the wood, 320- or 400-grit is usually sufficient.

Types of sanding

I used a variety of sanders for the projects in this book. Here are descriptions and recommendations.

Vertical sanders

Vertical sanders are efficient for sanding the outside of straight-sided bowls and leaving even walls. However, they may leave vertical scratches that must be sanded out. To sand the bowl, tilt the table to the desired angle and rotate as you sand to avoid flat spots. If the rings glued up unevenly, you may need to complete the process using a flexible pad sander to avoid removing too much wood at the top or the bottom of the rings.

Spindle sanders

Spindle sanders are used to sand the inside surface of straight-sided bowls before the bottom is added. Tilt the table to the appropriate angle and be sure the bowl contacts the spindle only at that angle. Check your work frequently to be sure you are leaving enough wood at the bottom for gluing on the base. Spindle sanders are also used to contour the necks of vases and to shape pedestals.

Flexible pad sanders

Flexible pad sanders are the least expensive tools for sanding bowl interiors. They are also used for contouring bowl lips and bases, and for sanding the outer surface of bowls. These sanders chuck into a drill, drill press, or flexible shaft, and use sanding discs that attach with a hook and loop system. They come in soft and standard densities.

Standard density pads are used for shaping, and with a light touch, can also be used for final sanding.

Inflatable ball sander

This innovative and highly recommended tool inflates with a small pump, and is invaluable for contouring the inside surfaces of bowls, especially those with flutes or petals. Although not cheap, it is sturdy and extremely effective. If you make many bowls, you will find the investment worthwhile. Several grits, from coarse to fine, are available as sleeves that fit over the inflatable unit.

Detail sanders

These small random orbit sanders are useful for removing swirl marks and evening out irregularities on the outside face of square and rectangular bowls.

Sanding mops

Sanding mops can be used to smooth the surface of the bowl before applying the finish, to soften edges, and to reveal rough or uneven spots that need further sanding. They can also be used to smooth the surface after applying the first coat of shellac. I use a 320-grit mop for this purpose.

Hand sanding

There is no substitute for hand sanding to smooth curved edges or to remove unwanted scratches. 220 grit is a good choice for final shaping and removal of scratches and glue spots, followed by progressive sanding, up to 320 or 400, depending on the type of wood. A 320-grit sanding sponge or 0000 steel wool (either regular or synthetic) works well to smooth the finish between coats.

Applying the Finish

Before applying the finish, wipe the bowl with mineral spirits to reveal glue spots. Sand them off. Any spots you miss can be removed after the first coat of finish is applied.

Selecting a finishing material

If the bowl is primarily decorative, Danish oil, shellac, or polyurethane are all suitable finishing materials, depending on the look desired. Certain woods, however, such as aspen, look much better with a glossy finish.

For a bowl that will get a lot of use, Danish oil and shellac are preferable, because they are easier than polyurethane to repair when worn.

None of these finishes are considered toxic once fully cured. Shellac cures quickly; bowls using other finishes should not be considered non-toxic until the odor fully dissipates.

If you're concerned about food safety, use an oil made for butcher block or salad bowls, or mix blonde, non-waxed shellac flakes with pure grain (not denatured) alcohol.

Applying spray shellac

I've used shellac for most of the bowls in this book. I prefer to apply it by spraying, rather than brushing, given the small size of the bowls. The first coat acts as a sealer. It may also raise the grain and reveal missed glue spots that need to be sanded off. Sand off any roughness with 0000 steel wool or synthetic equivalent, a sanding mop with 320 grit, or a 320-grit sanding sponge. Remove sanding particles with a shop vacuum, making sure to cover the nozzle with a soft cloth to avoid scratches. Wipe the piece with a tack cloth, damp cloth, or damp paper towel to remove any remaining particles. Apply several coats of shellac, sanding smooth between them, until you reach the depth of finish you want. To get a good coating without drips or sags, elevate the project, hold the can upright, and spray with sweeping strokes. Avoid starting or stopping the stroke on the bowl. To spray the outside of a bowl with steep sides, invert it over a tall spray can.

Applying Danish oil

Danish oil gives a low luster and accentuates the grain. Apply at least three or four coats, more if desired, until a soft sheen is achieved. Apply oil liberally, let it set for about thirty minutes, then wipe it off. Allow about one day's drying time between coats, and rub off any roughness with 0000 steel wool. After the oil has fully dried, (several days, depending on weather) you can rub out the finish with 0000 steel wool and paste wax.

It's now time to move on to Chapter Two, which starts with a step-by-step guide to the creation of the Basic Bowl.

Basic Stacked Bowls

All of the projects in this book consist of a series of rings, cut at an angle, glued up, and sanded. Even vases are just several series of rings. This means that the techniques and principles used are essentially the same whether your project is simple or complex. The difficulty of your project depends upon several factors: choice of wood, cutting angles, bowl shape, and whether lamination is used.

The projects in this chapter introduce two different methods to guide your cuts: the pattern method and the ring method. The pattern method uses a paper pattern consisting of an outline and a series of two to five concentric rings. Having a pattern for each ring helps maintain the shape of the bowl, but doesn't allow adjustment for slight cutting irregularities. The first four bowls in this chapter use the pattern method.

The ring method uses a paper pattern consisting of an outline and first ring only. Each ring, when cut, forms the pattern for the next, resulting in a more precise alignment than possible with the pattern method. Since the shape of each ring depends on the one cut before it, accurate cutting is critical. The ring method must be used with bowls requiring cutting of multiple angles or that require inserts of contrasting wood, but it can be used with any bowl. The last bowl in this chapter, the Scrolled-Top Bowl, introduces the ring method.

The chapter starts with a step-by-step construction of a basic round bowl, and will familiarize you with basic techniques. Once you're comfortable with the basics, you can try other shapes and learn how to add interest and variety to your work.

The bowls in this chapter are created by a series of angled rings that are stacked, glued together, and sanded.

The first bowl I ever made was cut from aspen. Aspen is soft and inexpensive, which makes it a low-risk choice for a first bowl. If you've never worked with aspen, you'll be surprised at how attractive it is when sanded well and shellacked.

Materials and Tools

Wood
* (1) 8" x 8" x ¾" (203mm x 203mm x 19mm) aspen or other wood that is easy to cut

Materials
* Packing tape (optional)
* Glue
* Repositionable adhesive
* Sanding discs for flexible pad sander, assorted grits 60 to 400
* Sandpaper for inflatable ball sander, assorted grits 60 to 320 (optional)
* Sandpaper for hand sanding, assorted grits 220 to 400

* 0000 steel wool or 320-grit sanding sponge
* Spray shellac

Tools
* Scroll saw blade, size #9
* Drill bit size #54 or ¹⁄₁₆" (2mm)
* Awl
* Ruler
* Bowl press or clamps
* 2" (51mm) flexible pad sander
* Inflatable ball sander and pump (optional)

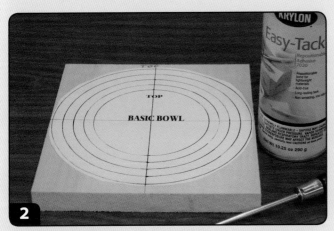

1

Drawing the guidelines. Draw two intersecting lines through the middle of the bowl blank. These form guidelines that help you align the rings properly when gluing up the bowl. Mark the top of the blank.

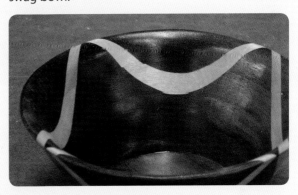

2

Aligning the pattern. Make a copy of the pattern from page 27. Apply the repositionable adhesive. Puncture the middle point of the pattern with an awl, and place the point of the awl at the intersection of the two lines on the wood. Line up the guidelines on the pattern with the guidelines on the wood and press the pattern into place.

Guidelines

It's important to draw guidelines and other orienting marks to maintain alignment. Proper alignment of grain makes the bowl look as though it were constructed from a single piece of wood, and gives the illusion of continuity to laminations. Sometimes misalignments are barely noticeable. Unfortunately, that was not true of this mahogany swag bowl.

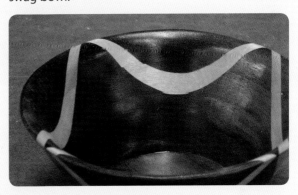

To tape or not to tape

Many scrollers use packing tape over or under patterns, or blue painter's tape under patterns, to lubricate the blade while cutting. I've found that certain hard woods, like cherry, are much more likely to burn without tape, while softer woods, like mahogany, do fine without it. If you're not sure what to do, try a test cut to see if it's worth the extra step.

3

Cutting the outline. Tilt the table of your scroll saw to 28°, left side down. Use a #9 blade, tensioned tightly, to cut clockwise along the outmost line. Let the blade cut freely to avoid distortion and keep the proper angle. Remove bowl from waste.

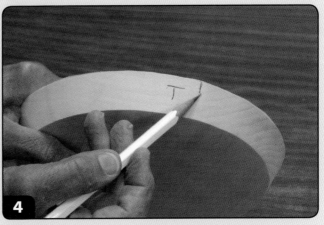

4

Marking the top. Mark the top of the bowl on the outer face of the blank. This will help keep the rings oriented when you glue them up. Extend each of the four guidelines onto the outer face of the blank.

Chapter Two: Basic Stacked Bowls

5

Drilling the entry holes. If using a hand drill or rotary tool, mark all entry holes with an awl to prevent the bit from slipping. Place a 28° angle guide so it faces the center of the blank. Drill all entry holes with a #54 or ¹⁄₁₆" (2mm) bit.

Alternative for drilling entry holes

If you don't have the correct angle guide at hand, you can use the scrap from your first cut as an angle guide. Or, if you have a drill press with a tilting table, you can set the table to 28° and drill the entry holes, angling them toward the center of the blank.

6

7

Completing the first ring. Insert the blade through the outermost hole and cut clockwise along the pattern line to complete the first ring. Place the ring on top of the remainder of the bowl blank. Transfer the guidelines from the pattern to the inside face of the cut ring. Extend guidelines from the top of the ring onto the inner and outer edges.

Cutting the second, third, and fourth rings. Insert the blade through the next entry hole and cut out the second ring as in Step 6. Mark the top and extend all guidelines. Repeat for the third and fourth rings. Each should line up with the previous ring.

8

9

Stacking the rings. Stack the rings, keeping the tops oriented, and match up step guideline extensions. Extend the marks from ring to ring on both the inside and outside surfaces so you can re-align them easily.

Preparing for gluing. Erase all guidelines on the top face of the rings to prevent them from appearing as tiny dots on the sides of the bowl. Stack the rings and hold the stacked bowl up to the light. Look for spaces between rings. If you find any, sand the ring faces smooth until the spaces disappear.

Wooden Bowls from the Scroll Saw

Testing and adjusting the angle

Every project in this book includes recommended cutting angles. These angles are based on two factors: thickness of the wood and width of the ring. Wood that is thicker or thinner than specified or a table tilt that is "off" will result in rings not lining up as well as they should. Before cutting any bowl, you might want to test the suggested cutting angle, using wood the same thickness as your bowl, to be sure it works for you. Follow the steps below to make an angle tester and test the angle.

If your cut was not accurate, try a tighter blade tension and take extra care not to distort the blade while cutting.

If your cutting angle was accurate and the ring hangs over the edge of the base by more than a small amount, increase the table angle by one or two degrees. If the ring sits inside the base by more than a small amount, reduce the table angle by one or two degrees. To counter the forces of gravity when cutting at a steep angle, be sure to keep the wood pushed up against the blade.

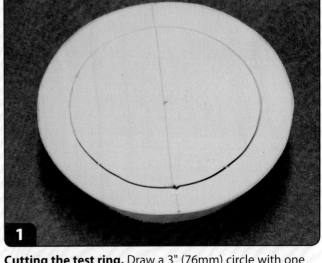

1

Cutting the test ring. Draw a 3" (76mm) circle with one ring the same width as your bowl's rings. Cut the ring as though it were a bowl.

2

Checking the alignment. Place the ring on top of the base and see how well it lines up. If your angle is correct, the two pieces should be closely aligned.

3

Checking the angle of the cut. If the pieces are not well aligned, check to see if your ring was cut at the intended angle. Do this by holding the ring next to the blade and see if the two line up.

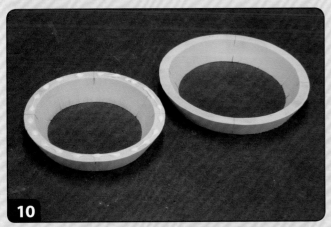

10

Gluing the rings. Set the base aside. It will be glued on in Step 13. Stack the rings and do a final check for alignment. Starting with the smallest ring, dot the top of the ring with glue. Spread the glue, covering surfaces thoroughly. Press the next ring firmly into place. Check alignment and adjust rings if necessary. Repeat for the remaining rings.

11

Using the bowl press. Place the glued-up rings in the bowl press, using wax paper above and below the rings. Tighten the wing nuts alternately, as you would on a car wheel, exerting firm but not excessive pressure. Let dry for a few minutes, unclamp, and clean up any glue squeeze-out. Re-clamp and let dry thoroughly.

12

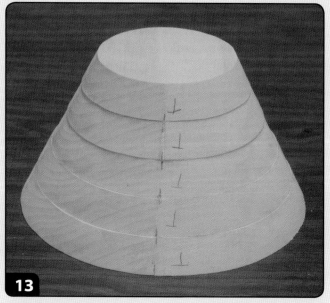

13

Sanding the bowl interior. Use a spindle sander with the table set to 28°. Be sure the bowl contacts the spindle only at this angle. You can also use an inflatable ball or flexible pad sander. Be sure the inside of the bottom ring is round—it cannot be corrected after attaching the base. The bottom of the smallest ring should be at least ¼" (6mm) wide for gluing to the base.

Gluing on the base. Sand the top of the base smooth and glue it to the bottom ring using the bowl press. Let it sit for about five minutes, then remove it from the press and clean excess glue from the inside bottom surface as thoroughly as possible. Return to press, and let dry.

26

14

15

Sanding the outside. Use a vertical belt sander or flexible pad sander to sand off all irregularities. Use progressively finer grits until the bowl is smooth. Re-sand inner surfaces if necessary. Try to keep the width of the top rim even. Round off the edges of the top ring and base.

Applying the finish. Apply mineral spirits to the bowl to reveal glue spots. Mark any with a white pencil or chalk. When the bowl is dry, sand off the glue spots. Apply the first coat of shellac and let dry. Smooth the surface with a 320-grit sanding sponge or 0000 steel wool. Vacuum, wipe with a damp cloth or paper towel, then recoat. Repeat until desired finish is obtained.

Alternate version

To make the alternate version of the basic bowl, you will need to make the following changes to the materials and instructions:

- Wood is ½" (13mm) zebrawood, not ¾" (19mm) aspen
- Outer circle is 7¼" (184mm), not 7" (178mm)
- Cutting angle is 38°, not 28°
- Base is inverted and thinned to about ¼" (6mm)

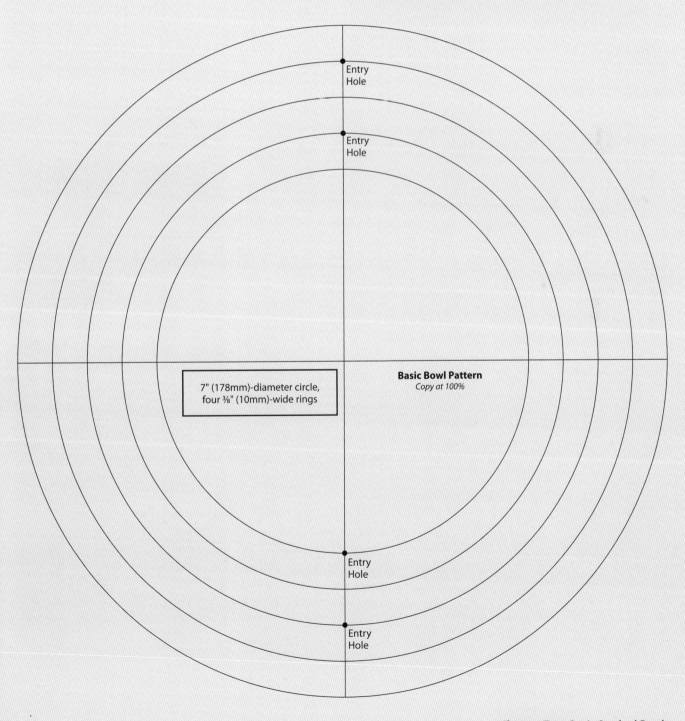

Entry Hole

Entry Hole

7" (178mm)-diameter circle, four ⅜" (10mm)-wide rings

Basic Bowl Pattern
Copy at 100%

Entry Hole

Entry Hole

Creating contour with freehand sanding

Freehand sanding serves a number of different purposes. At its most basic, it lets you achieve a smooth and even finish. As a technique for shaping, it mimics the effect of cutting tools on lathe-turned bowls by removing wood selectively to create interesting angles and curves. Bowl sanders can be used with a drill, drill press, or flexible shaft. I prefer using a drill press since it leaves my hands free to rotate the bowl. Much sawdust will be generated, so be sure to wear a dust mask, use eye protection, and vacuum your work and work area frequently.

If you've never done freehand sanding, it may take a while to feel comfortable with the equipment. If you use a light touch and check your work frequently, you're not likely to create a problem you can't correct. Proper technique depends on whether you are sanding the inside or outside of the bowl, and whether you are shaping aggressively or trying to achieve a smooth, even finish.

In general, it is important to hold the bowl tightly, move it against the direction of rotation of the sander, and keep light but even pressure. Unless you've already done a preliminary straight sanding, start with a coarse grit for shaping, and move to progressively finer ones to achieve a smooth finish. The coarser the grit is, the more pronounced the sanding marks will be—try starting with 100 grit, moving to 80 or 60 only if you need more cutting power. Once the bowl is shaped, use a light touch to avoid distortion. For ease of access, most inside sanding is done before gluing on the bottom; be careful not to catch the sander on the lower edge. Be aware of the contour you are trying to achieve, and check your work frequently.

Inner surfaces

Inflatable ball sanders are invaluable for sanding petals, flutes, and reaching lower rings in tall bowls. They can also be used on flat surfaces if you keep the work moving to avoid creating ridges. Short brushing strokes work well to smooth the sides.

Flexible pad sanders can be used on all but the narrowest parts of bowl interiors. The 2" (51mm) size with a pad of standard density is the most versatile, but a 1½" (38mm) pad may be needed to sand areas with small diameters. Short, light strokes help maintain control.

Shaping a lip with an outward flare

To shape an outward flare, hold the bowl securely with both hands and use short inside-to-outside strokes against the upper edge. Be careful to avoid distortion once the desired shape is achieved. Hand sanding will smooth out minor irregularities.

Use inflatable ball sanders to sand interiors.

Use inside-to-outside strokes to shape the lip's outward flare.

Contouring the base

Use a 2" (51mm) flexible pad sander to smooth and shape the outside, stroking the bowl lightly to avoid ridges. Once the base is attached, it can be contoured by holding the bowl upside-down and sanding away material at the lower edge until the desired shape is achieved.

The base can be contoured after being glued to the bowl.

A beginner makes a bowl

To make sure my instructions for the basic bowl were easy to follow, I asked a novice scroller to construct a bowl and indicate where instructions were not clear.

His glued up bowl looked a little rough, but once sanded and finished was quite impressive.

29

Eight-Petal Bowl

Petal-shaped bowls of various configurations are found throughout this book. An inflatable ball sander is highly recommended for bowls of this type to keep the flutes nicely shaped and even. If you don't have one, a flexible pad sander in the 1½" (38mm) size can be used for the bowl insides. Since a great deal of shaping is involved, save the denser woods for other projects and use an easy-to-sand wood like mahogany or walnut. Take your time when sanding the bowl and check the shape frequently to be sure the petals remain equal in size.

Materials and Tools

Wood
- (1) 8" x 8" x ¾" (203mm x 203mm x 19mm) walnut or other wood that is easy to cut and sand

Materials
- Packing tape (optional)
- Glue
- Repositionable adhesive
- Sanding discs for flexible pad sander, assorted grits 60 to 400
- Sandpaper for inflatable ball sander, assorted grits 60 to 320 (optional)
- Sandpaper for hand sanding, assorted grits 220 to 400
- 0000 steel wool or 320-grit sanding sponge
- Spray shellac or Danish oil

Tools
- Scroll saw blade, size #9
- Drill bit size #54 or ¹⁄₁₆" (2mm)
- Awl
- Ruler
- Bowl press or clamps
- 2" (51mm) flexible pad sander
- Inflatable ball sander and pump (optional) or 1½" (38mm) flexible pad sander

Making the bowl

1. Draw guidelines on the bowl blank.

2. Attach the pattern with repositionable adhesive.

3. Tilt the table 28°, left side down.

4. Cut the bowl outline in a clockwise direction.

5. Mark the top of the outer rim.

6. Drill 28° entry holes and cut out three rings.

7. Mark the top and draw guidelines on each ring.

8. Stack the rings. Check for alignment and spaces.

9. Glue the rings, clamp them, and let dry.

10. Sand the inside of the bowl smooth.

11. Glue on the base, clamp, and let dry.

12. Shape the outside of bowl.

13. Apply finish of choice.

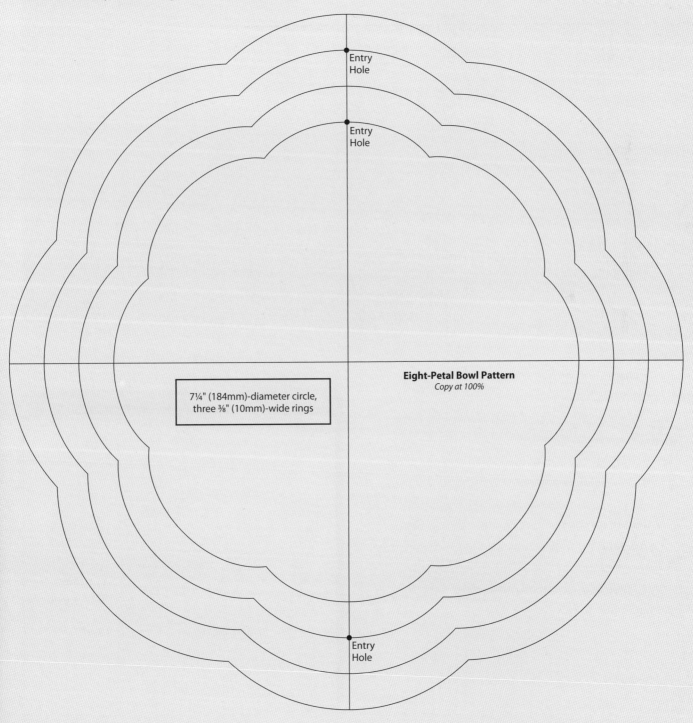

Entry Hole

Entry Hole

Entry Hole

7¼" (184mm)-diameter circle, three ⅜" (10mm)-wide rings

Eight-Petal Bowl Pattern
Copy at 100%

The rounded square is a practical and useful shape for a bowl. Its uncluttered lines also make it the perfect showcase for a special piece of wood. I decided to use a piece of teak I had rescued from a storage shed. Despite teak's reputation for being hard to glue and finish because of its high oil content, I had no problem treating it as any other wood. However, its high silica content (which gives it a non-skid quality for decking) makes it highly abrasive, so if you use teak, be prepared to change blades frequently.

Materials and Tools

Wood
- (1) 8" x 8" x ¾" (203mm x 203mm x 19mm) teak or wood of choice

Materials
- Packing tape (optional)
- Glue
- Repositionable adhesive
- Sanding discs for flexible pad sander, assorted grits 60 to 400
- Sandpaper for inflatable ball sander, assorted grits 60 to 320 (optional)
- Sandpaper for hand sanding, assorted grits 220 to 400

- 0000 steel wool or 320-grit sanding sponge
- Spray shellac or Danish oil

Tools
- Scroll saw blade, size #9
- Drill bit size #54 or ¹⁄₁₆" (2mm)
- Awl
- Ruler
- Bowl press or clamps
- 2" (51mm) flexible pad sander
- Inflatable ball sander and pump (optional)

Making the bowl

1. Draw guidelines on the bowl blank.

2. Attach the pattern.

3. Tilt the table 28°, left side down.

4. Cut the bowl outline in a clockwise direction.

5. Mark the top of the outer rim.

6. Drill 28° entry holes and cut out three rings.

7. Mark the top and draw guidelines on each ring.

8. Stack the rings. Check for alignment and spaces.

9. Glue the rings, clamp them, and let dry.

10. Sand the inside of the bowl smooth.

11. Glue on the base, clamp, and let dry.

12. Shape the outside of bowl.

13. Apply finish of choice.

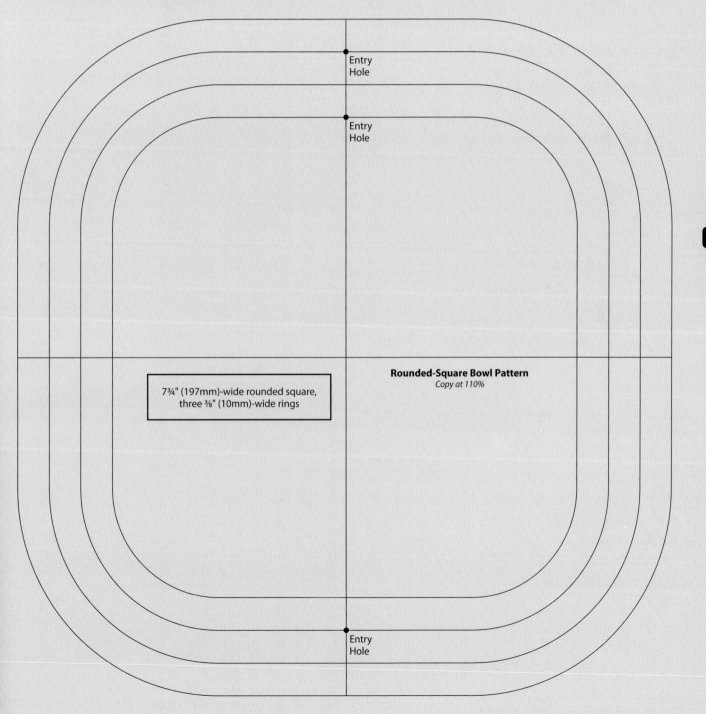

Entry Hole

Entry Hole

7¾" (197mm)-wide rounded square, three ⅜" (10mm)-wide rings

Rounded-Square Bowl Pattern
Copy at 110%

Entry Hole

33

Wavy Bowl, ipé.

34

This graceful bowl is a variation of the Eight-Petal bowl, with gentle curves and a fluid outline. After making the bowl in maple, I tried the same pattern with a piece of attractively grained ipé I had picked up on the "shorts" pile at a lumberyard (see photo above). This extremely dense wood is normally used for decks and lathe-turned pens, and I had second thoughts about even trying to use it. To my surprise, the wood was possible to cut and shape without too much difficulty, and took on an amazing sheen with the first coat of shellac. I left the walls and rim fairly wide to match the dense feel of the bowl.

Materials and Tools

Wood
- ❖ (1) 8" x 8" x ¾" (203mm x 203mm x 19mm) maple or wood of your choice

Materials
- ❖ Packing tape (optional)
- ❖ Glue
- ❖ Repositionable adhesive
- ❖ Sanding discs for flexible pad sander, assorted grits 60 to 400
- ❖ Sandpaper for inflatable ball sander, assorted grits 60 to 320 (optional)
- ❖ Sandpaper for hand sanding, assorted grits 220 to 400

- ❖ 0000 steel wool or 320-grit sanding sponge
- ❖ Spray shellac or Danish oil

Tools
- ❖ Scroll saw blade, size #9
- ❖ Drill bit size #54 or ¹⁄₁₆" (2mm)
- ❖ Awl
- ❖ Ruler
- ❖ Bowl press or clamps
- ❖ 2" (51mm) flexible pad sander
- ❖ Inflatable ball sander and pump (optional)

Making the bowl

1. Draw guidelines on the bowl blank.

2. Attach the pattern with repositionable adhesive.

3. Tilt the table 28°, left side down.

4. Cut the bowl outline in a clockwise direction.

5. Mark the top of the outer rim.

6. Drill 28° entry holes and cut out three rings.

7. Mark the top and draw guidelines on each ring.

8. Stack the rings. Check for alignment and spaces.

9. Glue the rings, clamp them, and let dry.

10. Sand the inside of the bowl smooth.

11. Glue on the base, clamp, and let dry.

12. Shape the outside of bowl.

13. Apply finish of choice.

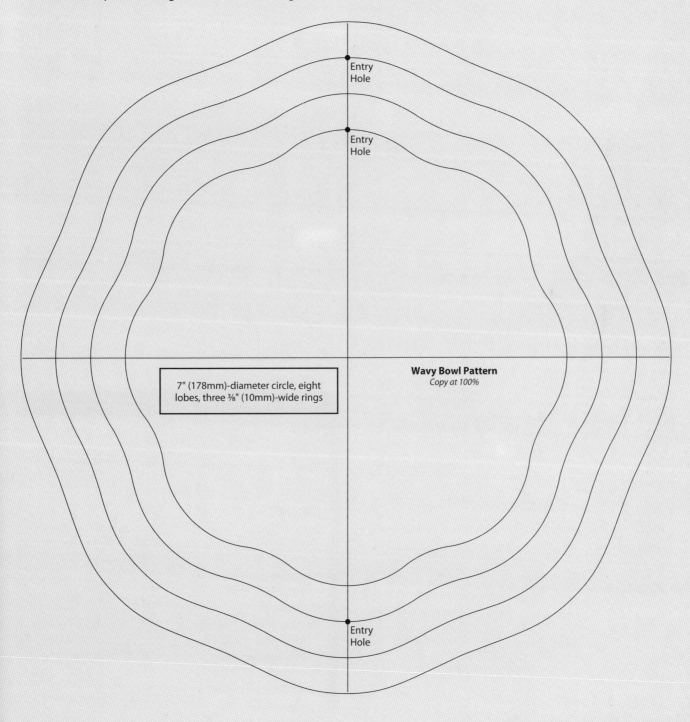

Entry Hole

Entry Hole

Entry Hole

7" (178mm)-diameter circle, eight lobes, three ⅜" (10mm)-wide rings

Wavy Bowl Pattern
Copy at 100%

35

Scrolled-Top Bowl

I decided to end this chapter with a bowl that could not be more different from the Basic Bowl. It highlights how much variety can be obtained from the basic round pattern. I modeled this project after a lathe-turned bowl I bought several years ago at a crafts show. The free-form edge is cut after the bowl is completed, and the base is sharply contoured by sanding. To obtain the desired effect, the bowl must be sufficiently tall to allow for cutting the curve, and the sides must be of uniform thickness.

Materials and Tools

Wood
❖ (1) 8" x 8" x ¾" (203mm x 203mm x 19mm) maple or wood of your choice

Materials
❖ Packing tape (optional)
❖ Glue
❖ Repositionable adhesive
❖ Sanding discs for flexible pad sander, assorted grits 60 to 400
❖ Sandpaper for inflatable ball sander, assorted grits 60 to 320 (optional)
❖ Sandpaper for hand sanding (220 to 400)

❖ 0000 steel wool or 320-grit sanding sponge
❖ Spray shellac or Danish oil

Tools
❖ Scroll saw blade, size #9
❖ Spiral blade #3 (optional)
❖ Drill bit size #54 or ¹⁄₁₆" (2mm)
❖ Awl
❖ Ruler
❖ Bowl press or clamps
❖ 2" (51mm) flexible pad sander
❖ Inflatable ball sander and pump (optional)

Because the ¼" (6mm)-wide rings that are needed don't allow much extra wood for correcting irregularities, an alternative cutting approach, the ring method, is used. This method, where each ring is used as the model for the one that follows it, produces a more precise alignment than the pattern method. Patterns for bowls cut with the ring method consist of an outline and cutting guide for the first ring. The following instructions are for a five-ring bowl cut at a 20° angle, but the procedure is the same regardless of the number of rings or cutting angle. The ring method is used in later chapters for bowls with inserts of different colored woods, and for bowls requiring more than one cutting angle.

Making the bowl

1. Draw guidelines on the blank and attach the pattern with repositionable adhesive.

2. Cut the first ring with the saw table tilted at 20°, left side down, cutting the outline in a clockwise direction.

3. Drill a 20° entry hole and complete the first ring. Remove the pattern.

4. Place the ring on top of the blank, keeping guidelines aligned, and transfer the guidelines from the blank to the ring. Keeping the ring in place, trace the inside of the ring on the bowl blank to form the pattern for the second ring (see photo, right). Mark the top of the ring.

5. Drill a 20° entry hole for the second ring and cut out the second ring at a 20° angle, table tilted left side down, cutting clockwise.

6. Cut the remaining three rings in the same way, transferring guidelines to each ring as it is cut. There will be five rings when you are done.

7. Stack the rings. Check for alignment and spaces.

8. Glue the rings, clamp them, and let dry.

9. Sand the inside of the bowl smooth.

10. Glue on the base, clamp, and let dry.

11. Shape the outside of the bowl, contouring the base steeply.

12. Attach the top pattern to the inside of the bowl with adhesive. You will probably need to make some adjustments to achieve a good fit.

Step 4

Trace the inside of the ring on the blank.

Making the bowl (continued)

13. Begin cutting at the top of the bowl. Rotate the bowl to get as much clearance as possible (see photo, right).

14. When you can cut no further, back out and cut off the waste, cutting from the top of the bowl inward. Continue cutting, removing waste to permit access (see photo below). Work your way around the bowl in this manner until you can resume cutting normally. If you cannot cut as deeply as needed with a regular blade, deepen the cut with a spindle sander, or use a spiral blade.

15. When the cut is complete, sand the edge smooth.

16. Apply finish of choice.

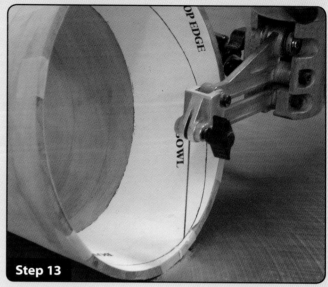

Step 13

Scroll the edge.

Cutting

For rings to align perfectly, the bottom of the first ring must match the top of the second ring, and so on. Using each ring as the pattern for the next usually gives a more precise alignment than using a paper pattern. However, if any ring is substantially miscut, all that follow will be misshapen. To prevent this from happening, check the shape of each ring after it is cut, and make corrections in the outline of the next ring if necessary.

Step 14

Cut off the waste if needed.

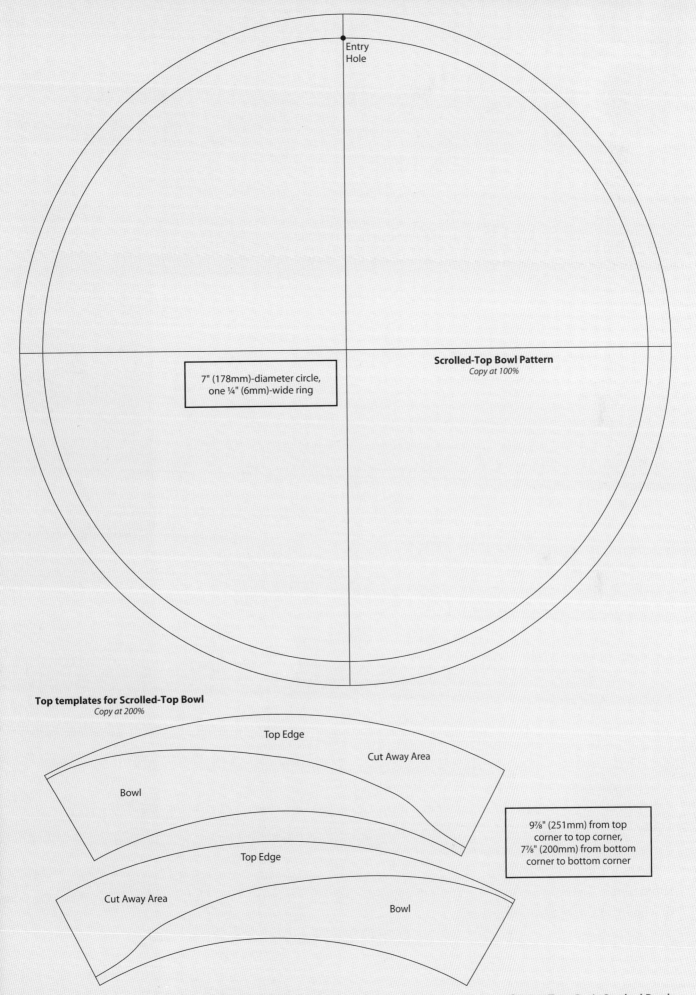

Entry
Hole

Scrolled-Top Bowl Pattern
Copy at 100%

7" (178mm)-diameter circle,
one ¼" (6mm)-wide ring

Top templates for Scrolled-Top Bowl
Copy at 200%

Top Edge

Cut Away Area

Bowl

9⅞" (251mm) from top
corner to top corner,
7⅞" (200mm) from bottom
corner to bottom corner

Top Edge

Cut Away Area

Bowl

Chapter Two: Basic Stacked Bowls

3

Laminated Wood Bowls

Creating a laminated wood bowl on the scroll saw is an exciting process—swags, curves, and interesting patterns of various kinds emerge unexpectedly from flat pieces of wood. There are two different ways of creating laminated bowls. The first is by gluing up stock to produce a bowl blank that consists of two or more different woods, combined in various ways. The second is by using a regular, non-laminated bowl blank, and inserting rings of different woods and colors during the bowl-cutting process. The bowls in this chapter are based on the first method: gluing up wood to create a laminated blank.

Although the cutting and gluing process for making laminated bowls is similar to that used for single-wood bowls, there are three main differences.

First, the laminated blank must be sanded flat so that the rings will stack properly for gluing. If much sanding is needed, this may result in a blank that is thinner than specified. If there is much of a deviation, the cutting angle must be increased to compensate. You can either compute a new cutting angle (page 134) or cut a test ring from scrap wood of the same thickness as the sanded blank (see page 25).

Second, wood is often not milled exactly to the thickness specified by the seller. If the blank is formed from several pieces of wood that are stacked and glued, small deviations and multiple glue layers can add up and affect the final thickness. Here too, the solution is to measure the thickness and determine the correct angle by computation or by cutting test rings.

And finally, laminated patterns require precise alignment during glue-up to maintain the continuity of the pattern.

The bowls in this chapter represent a sampling of different types of laminations. They are fun to make, and a good way to use up scraps of wood you can't bear to throw away.

The bowls in this chapter were created by gluing up stock to produce a bowl blank with multiple woods.

Intersecting swags of different colors add elegance to this simple round bowl. The step-by-step instructions will guide you through the multi-step lamination. Once the bowl blank is glued up and sanded, the bowl is completed like a single-wood bowl.

Materials and Tools

Wood
- ❖ (1) 7" x 4½" x ¾" (178mm x 114mm x 19mm) mahogany
- ❖ (2) 7" x ¾" x ¾" (178mm x 19mm x 19mm) mahogany
- ❖ (2) 7" x ½" x ¾" (178mm x 13mm x 19mm) purpleheart
- ❖ (4) 4½" x ¾" x ¼" (114mm x 19mm x 6mm) yellowheart

Materials
- ❖ Packing tape (optional)
- ❖ Glue
- ❖ Sanding discs for flexible pad sander, assorted grits 60 to 400
- ❖ Sandpaper for inflatable ball sander, assorted grits 60 to 320 (optional)
- ❖ Sandpaper for hand sanding, assorted grits 220 to 400
- ❖ 0000 steel wool or 320-grit sanding sponge
- ❖ Spray shellac or Danish oil

Tools
- ❖ Scroll saw blade, size #9
- ❖ Drill bit size #54 or ¹⁄₁₆" (2mm)
- ❖ Ruler
- ❖ Compass
- ❖ Bowl press or clamps
- ❖ Clamps for lamination
- ❖ 2" (51mm) flexible pad sander
- ❖ Inflatable ball sander and pump (optional)

1

Attach the mahogany and purpleheart. Glue up the three pieces of mahogany and two pieces of purpleheart in this order: ¾" (19mm) mahogany, purpleheart, 4½" (114mm) mahogany, purpleheart, ¾" (19mm) mahogany. Clamp and let dry overnight. Trim, if necessary, to form a 7" (178mm) square.

2

Divide the blank. Draw intersecting guidelines across the blank. The center point should be 3½" (89mm) from each side. Make a mark ¼" (6mm) on each side of the end points of the guidelines. You will have eight marks. Connect the marks as shown to form corner triangles.

3

Attach the yellowheart. Cut off the triangles, marking each triangle and its adjacent side so you can reposition it properly. Sand all of the cut sides flat. Glue two pieces of yellowheart on opposite sides of the blank, ¼" (6mm) side up. The strips should sit flat against the blank. Clamp, using pieces of wood to avoid damaging the sides, and let dry. Glue the remaining pieces of yellowheart in the same manner.

4

Attach the corners. Glue two opposite corners onto the corresponding sides of the blank. Clamp and let dry. Use a straight edge to be sure the purpleheart strips are aligned properly, and be careful the pieces don't shift. Glue the remaining two corners in the same manner.

5

Sand the blank. Use a sanding drum or hand sander to sand the blank smooth. Redraw the guidelines if they have been sanded away.

Drawing a pattern directly on wood

To guarantee precise pattern placement on a complex lamination, circular patterns can easily be drawn directly on the bowl blank. Here's how:

Draw guidelines on the bowl blank, centering them on the lamination. Measuring from the center point, mark a point on one of the guidelines that is half the bowl's diameter. Position the point of your compass at the intersection of the guidelines and draw a circle the same as the diameter of your bowl. Using the same center point, draw a second circle inside the first so that the distance between the two circles is the same as the width of the ring you will be cutting.

43

Chapter Three: Laminated Wood Bowls

1

Drawing the outline and first ring. Mark a point on one of the guidelines that is 3¼" (83mm) from the center of the circle. Use your compass and that mark to draw a circle 6½" (165mm) in diameter. Mark a point on one of the guidelines that is ⅜" (10mm) inside this circle. Use your compass to draw a smaller circle that forms the inside edge of the first ring.

2

Cutting the first ring. Tilt the scroll saw table to an angle of 28°, left side down. Using a #9 blade, cut clockwise along the outer circle. Mark the top on the outside of the ring and extend guidelines down the sides.

3

Finishing the first ring. Use an angle guide or drill press with a tilting table to drill a 28° entry hole on the inner ring with a #54 or ¹⁄₁₆" (2mm) drill bit, pointed toward the center of the blank. Insert the blade through the entry hole and cut on the inner line to complete the first ring.

4

Marking and cutting the second ring. Place the ring you just cut on the bowl blank and align using the guidelines. Mark the top. Transfer the guidelines from the blank to the lower edge of the first ring. Keeping marks aligned, use the inside edge of the first ring to mark the cutting line for the second ring. Use the angle guide to drill an entry hole for the second ring directly opposite the top. (Alternating top and bottom makes the drill marks easier to sand out than if they were positioned directly behind each other.) Cut and mark the second ring. Use the second ring to draw the cutting line for the third ring.

5

Cutting the third ring. Cut and mark the third ring in the same way as the second.

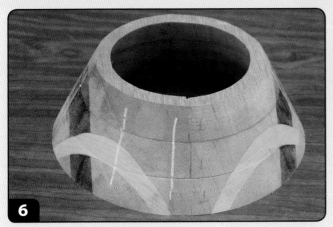

6

Preparing rings for gluing. Make sure all guidelines have been transferred to the sides of the rings. Erase any marks on the tops and lower edges of the rings. Stack and align the rings carefully. Draw lines down the side with a white pencil to help keep the alignment when gluing up. Check for spaces between the rings and sand flat if necessary.

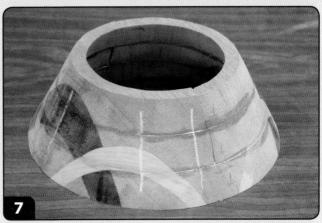

7

Gluing the rings. Set aside the base. It will be glued on in Step 9. Place dots of glue on the top of the third ring. Spread the glue evenly, covering the surface completely. Place the second ring on top, aligning carefully. Repeat the process for the first ring. Clamp the bowl with wax paper above and below the rings. After a few minutes, unclamp the bowl briefly and remove excess glue. Re-clamp and let dry.

8

Sanding the inside. Using a flexible pad sander or inflatable ball, sand the inside of the bowl. These tools give more flexibility for shaping than a spindle sander. Use progressively finer grits to sand the inside of the bowl smooth. Do a preliminary sanding of the outside with the flexible pad sander.

9

Gluing on the base. Align the base and glue it to the underside of the rings. Clamp the bowl. After a few minutes clean off glue residue on the inside of bowl. Re-clamp the bowl and let it dry.

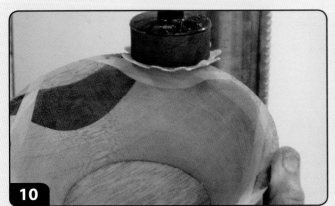

10

Sanding and shaping the outside and upper edge. Use the flexible pad sander to complete the sanding of the bowl, going from coarser to finer grits. Shape the lower edge and sand an outward flare on the upper edge to accentuate the swag. Check the bowl for shape and smoothness as you sand.

11

Finishing the bowl. Apply mineral spirits to the bowl to reveal any glue spots. Mark with a white pencil or chalk. When dry, sand off the glue spots. Apply the first coat of shellac and let it dry. Smooth the surface with a 320-grit sanding sponge or 0000 steel wool. Vacuum, remove the remaining particles with a damp cloth or paper towel, then recoat. Repeat until desired finish is obtained.

The plans for this bowl came about quite by accident. I was trying to make a colorful bowl with vertical stripes and inadvertently rotated one of the rings. Almost by magic, a basket weave pattern appeared. The effect was so compelling that I abandoned my original project and focused on ways to make the bowl look as much like a basket as possible. Because the laminated blank was fairly thick, I was able to use a smaller cutting angle to reduce the flare of the sides. Cutting four rings, rather than three, added to the bucket-like appearance, and a separate thin base yielded better proportions than a thick one.

Materials and Tools

Wood

Bowl:
- ❖ (1) 7½" x 7½" x ¾" (191mm x 191mm x 19mm) cedar
- ❖ (1) 7½" x 7½" x ¼" (191mm x 191mm x 6mm) padauk

Vertical strips:
- ❖ (3) 7½" x 1" x ¼" (191mm x 25mm x 6mm) poplar

Base:
- ❖ (1) 4½" x 4½" x ¼" (114mm x 114mm x 6mm) padauk

Materials
- ❖ Packing tape (optional)
- ❖ Glue
- ❖ Sanding discs for flexible pad sander, assorted grits 60 to 400
- ❖ Sandpaper for inflatable ball sander, assorted grits 60 to 320 (optional)
- ❖ Sandpaper for hand sanding, assorted grits 220 to 400
- ❖ 0000 steel wool or 320-grit sanding sponge
- ❖ Spray shellac or Danish oil

Tools
- ❖ Scroll saw blade, size #9
- ❖ Drill bit size #54 or ¹⁄₁₆" (2mm)
- ❖ Ruler
- ❖ Protractor
- ❖ Compass
- ❖ Bowl press or clamps
- ❖ Clamps for lamination
- ❖ 2" (51mm) flexible pad sander
- ❖ Inflatable ball sander and pump (optional)

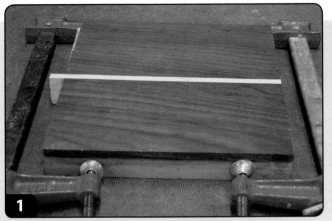

1

Glue the first strip. Glue the 7½" (191mm) piece of padauk to the cedar, keeping the grains running in the same direction. Clamp and let dry. Cut the blank in half along the grain. Smooth the cut edges. Glue the first poplar strip between the cut edges. Clamp and let dry.

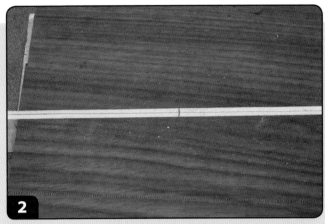

2

Mark the center of the first strip. Draw a line through the center of the poplar strip. Mark the center of the blank.

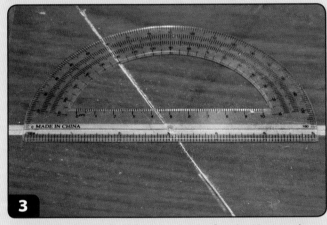

3

Draw the cutting line for the second strip. Center the protractor on the line drawn in Step 2. Use the protractor to mark a 60° angle. Draw a line through the blank at that angle.

4

Glue in the second strip. Cut the blank on the line drawn in Step 3. Smooth the cut edges. Glue the second poplar strip between the cut edges. Clamp and let dry. Draw a line through the center of the second strip. Mark a 60° angle in the same manner as the first strip. Cut on the line and smooth the edges.

5

Glue in the third strip. Glue in the third poplar strip. Clamp and let dry. Orient the blank so that the third strip is vertical and the V shapes formed by the first two pieces of poplar are directly opposite each other. Draw a line through the middle of the third strip. At the center point of the third strip, draw a line that is perpendicular to the line you just drew. This line should run through the center of the V shapes. These are your guidelines.

Note: Your blank is now divided into six segments. Don't be concerned about the apparent lack of alignment in the middle. The center piece left after the rings have been cut will be replaced by a solid piece of padauk to form the bottom of the bowl.

47

Chapter Three: Laminated Wood Bowls

Making the bowl

1. Using the center point on the poplar, draw a 7" (178mm)-diameter circle with a compass.

2. Draw a second circle ⅜" (10mm) inside the first circle.

3. Tilt scroll saw table 22°, left side down.

4. Cut the bowl outline in a clockwise direction.

5. Mark the top of the outer rim.

6. Drill a 22° entry hole and cut out the first ring.

7. Check ring alignment and adjust the angle if needed. Mark the top.

8. Use the inside of each ring to mark the outline for the next ring.

9. Cut three additional rings. Mark the top of each. The remaining piece of the blank will not be used.

10. Stack the rings. To create the basket weave effect, rotate each ring so the poplar strips are between the poplar strips of the ring below. Rings one and three should be aligned with each other, as should rings two and four.

11. Check for spaces.

12. Glue the rings, clamp them, and let dry.

13. Sand the inside of the bowl smooth.

14. Place the bowl on the remaining ¼" (6mm) piece of padauk and mark the outline of the bottom ring.

15. Tilt the saw table 22°, left side down, and cut the piece of padauk along the outline, cutting clockwise.

16. Glue this piece to the bottom of the rings to form the base. Clamp the bowl and let dry.

17. Sand the outside of the bowl and the upper edge.

18. Apply finish of choice.

Step 10

Align each ring so the poplar strips are located between the poplar strips of the ring below.

Working with padauk

I decided to use cedar as the primary wood, with padauk and poplar laminations. I loved the color combination, but found that the sanding dust from the padauk tended to settle into the soft surface of the cedar. I solved that problem by vacuuming frequently as I sanded, but discovered during finishing that if I wet the padauk too heavily with shellac, the orange color bled into the cedar. After sanding off the discoloration, I used very light coats and had no further problems. If you want to avoid this situation, replace the cedar with a denser or darker wood.

Alternate version

To make the alternate version of this bowl, you will need to make the following changes to the materials and instructions:

• Primary wood is ¾" (19mm) mahogany, not ¾" (19mm) cedar

48

Plaid Bowl

Fabrics are a good source of ideas for laminations. I was able to create a plaid effect by combining two lamination techniques: stacking and gluing layers of wood, and gluing in strips. The lamination, which is done in stages, is not difficult, but does require more wood than usual. However, I think the uniqueness of the bowl justifies the extra cost. I chose oak as the base wood because it contrasts well with purpleheart and maple. These woods are also of similar hardness, which facilitates sanding and finishing.

Materials and Tools

Wood

Bowl:
- (1) 8" x 8" x ½" (203mm x 203mm x 13mm) oak
- (1) 8" x 8" x ⅛" (203mm x 203mm x 3mm) maple
- (2) 8" x 8" x ⅛" (203mm x 203mm x 3mm) purpleheart

Strips:
- (8) 8" x 1" x ⅛" (203mm x 25mm x 3mm) purpleheart
- (4) 8" x 1" x ⅛" (203mm x 25mm x 3mm) maple

Note: The strips are cut slightly wide to allow for sanding the striped faces.

Base:
- (2) 6" x 6" x ⅛" (152mm x 152mm x 3mm) purpleheart
- (1) 6" x 6" x ⅛" (152mm x 152mm x 3mm) maple

Materials
- Packing tape (optional)
- Glue
- Sanding discs for flexible pad sander, assorted grits 60 to 400
- Sandpaper for inflatable ball sander, assorted grits 60 to 320 (optional)
- Sandpaper for hand sanding, assorted grits 220 to 400
- 0000 steel wool or 320-grit sanding sponge
- Spray shellac or Danish oil

Tools
- Scroll saw blade, size #9
- Drill bit size #54 or ¹⁄₁₆" (2mm)
- Ruler
- Compass
- Bowl press or clamps
- Clamps for lamination
- 2" (51mm) flexible pad sander
- Inflatable ball sander and pump (optional)

Chapter Three: Laminated Wood Bowls

1

Glue the blank. Glue the 8" x 8" (203mm x 203mm) pieces of wood in the following order: oak, purpleheart, maple, purpleheart. Be sure all grain runs in the same direction. Clamp and let dry.

2

Glue the strips. Glue the 8" x 1" x ⅛" (203mm x 25mm x 3mm) pieces of stock to make four separate strips. Each strip is glued in the following order: purpleheart, maple, purpleheart. Clamp and let dry. Sand the striped faces smooth.

3

Insert the first strip. Cut the 8" x 8" (203mm x 203mm) blank into two pieces, cutting with the grain. Each piece will measure 8" x 4" (203mm x 102mm). Sand the cut edges smooth. Glue one of the laminated strips, striped face up, between the two pieces. Check the edges of the blank to be sure the two halves are aligned. Clamp and let dry.

4

Insert the second strip. Cut the newly glued-up blank in half, this time cutting across the grain. Glue a second laminated strip between the halves. Check the alignment. Clamp and let dry.

5

Insert the third strip. Draw diagonal lines from corner to corner, passing through the center point. Cut along one of the diagonal lines. Sand the cut faces smooth. Glue the third laminated strip between the halves. Clamp and let dry.

6

Insert the fourth strip. Cut along the other diagonal line and repeat Step 5. Sand the top and bottom surfaces smooth with a drum or hand sander. Be sure the blank is flat and even. Because multiple layers of wood have been sandwiched, check the final thickness and adjust the cutting angle if needed.

Plaid Bowl

Making the bowl

1. With the purple side up, locate the center of the bowl blank. Please note all rings are cut on this side.

2. Draw a 7" (178mm)-diameter circle with a compass.

3. Draw a second circle ⅜" (10mm) inside the first circle.

4. Tilt the scroll saw table 24°, left side down.

5. Cut the outer circle in a clockwise direction.

6. Mark the top of the outer rim.

7. Drill a 24° entry hole and complete the first ring.

8. Check ring alignment and adjust the angle if needed. Mark the top.

9. Use the first ring to mark the outline for the second ring.

10. Cut the second ring. Mark and cut the third ring.

11. Stack the rings, checking for alignment and spaces.

12. Glue the rings, clamp them, and let dry.

13. Sand the inside of the bowl smooth.

14. Choose type of base, gluing pieces together if using the thin laminated base. (See sidebar, Choosing a base, right.)

15. Place the bowl on the base and mark the outline, if using the thin laminated base or the ¼" (6mm)-thick purpleheart base.

16. Cut the base at 24° if using the thin laminated base or the ¼" (6mm)-thick purpleheart base, saw table tilted left side down, cutting clockwise.

17. Glue on the base. Clamp and let dry.

18. Sand the outside of the bowl and upper edge.

19. Apply finish of choice.

Choosing a base

Different effects can be obtained by varying the type of base used for the bowl.

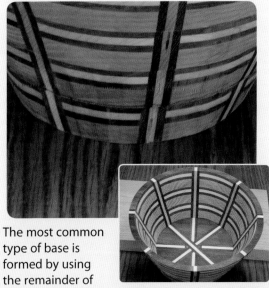

The most common type of base is formed by using the remainder of the bowl blank after cutting the rings. This choice continues the lamination pattern on both outside and inside the bowl.

A second choice is to laminate wood to produce a thinner matching base with a solid color face. To make this base, glue up the 6" (152mm) squares of ⅛" (3mm) purpleheart and maple, sandwiching the maple between the purpleheart.

A third choice is to use ¼" (6mm)-thick purpleheart.

51

Chapter Three: Laminated Wood Bowls

Gingham-patterned fabric was the inspiration for this bowl. The laminated inserts are quick and easy to do, and when glued into the bowl blank and cut at an angle, they form patterns that look remarkably like gingham checks. I chose a light background to highlight the laminations, but a darker wood would also work well.

Materials and Tools

Wood

Bowl:
- (1) 8" x 8" x ¾" (203mm x 203mm x 19mm) maple

A Strips:
- (2) 8" x 1½" x ¼" (203mm x 38mm x 6mm) purpleheart
- (1) 8" x 1½" x ¼" (203mm x 38mm x 6mm) cherry

B Strips:
- (2) 8" x ¾" x ¼" (203mm x 19mm x 6mm) cherry
- (1) 8" x ¾" x ¼" (203mm x 19mm x 6mm) oak

Materials
- Packing tape (optional)
- Glue
- Sanding discs for flexible pad sander, assorted grits 60 to 400
- Sandpaper for inflatable ball sander, assorted grits 60 to 320 (optional)
- Sandpaper for hand sanding, assorted grits 220 to 400
- 0000 steel wool or 320-grit sanding sponge
- Spray shellac or Danish oil

Tools
- Scroll saw blade, size #9
- Drill bit size #54 or ¹⁄₁₆" (2mm)
- Ruler
- Compass
- Bowl press or clamps
- Clamps for lamination
- 2" (51mm) flexible pad sander
- Inflatable ball sander and pump (optional)

Lamination guide

Glue up the strips. Glue up the pieces for strips A and B so that the contrasting piece is sandwiched between the other two. Clamp and let dry. Sand the striped faces smooth.

Complete the strips. Cut four ¼" (6mm) slices from the A strips, cutting parallel to the striped face. Cut two ¼" (6mm) slices from the B strips, cutting parallel to the striped face. Sandwich one B strip between two A strips. Glue and clamp them. Repeat with the remaining set of strips.

Glue in the strips. Cut the maple bowl blank in half along the grain. Sand the cut edges smooth. Insert one strip between the halves. Glue, clamp, and let dry. Cut the bowl blank in half across the grain. Sand the cut edges smooth. Insert the remaining strip between the halves, glue, clamp and let dry. Sand the laminated blank smooth.

Alternate version

To make the alternate version of this bowl, you will need to make the following changes to the materials and instructions:

- Outer circle is 6¾" (171mm), not 7" (178mm)

- Primary wood is ¾" (19mm) lacewood, not ¾" (19mm) maple

- Strip A is made of ¼" (6mm) maple and ¼" (6mm) oak, not ¼" (6mm) purpleheart and ¼" (6mm) cherry

- Strip B is made of ¼" (6mm) oak and ¼" (6mm) purpleheart, not ¼" (6mm) cherry and ¼" (6mm) oak

- Ring width is ½" (13mm) instead of ⅜" (10mm)

- Cutting angle is 34° instead of 28°

- 4 rings are cut, not 3

- Base is inverted and sanded to about ¼" (6mm)

Making the bowl

1. Locate the center of the bowl blank.

2. Draw a 7" (178mm)-diameter circle with a compass.

3. Draw a second circle ⅜" (10mm) inside the first circle.

4. Tilt the scroll saw table 28°, left side down.

5. Cut the bowl outline in a clockwise direction.

6. Mark the top of the outer rim.

7. Drill an entry hole at a 28° angle and cut out the first ring.

8. Mark the top of each ring.

9. Use the inside of each ring to mark the outline for the next ring.

10. Cut two additional rings, marking the top of each.

11. Stack the rings so that the laminated pieces are staggered.

12. Check for spaces between the rings.

13. Glue the rings, clamp them, and let dry.

14. Sand the inside of the bowl smooth.

15. Glue on the base, making sure to stagger the lamination. Clamp and let dry.

16. Sand the outside and upper edge of the bowl.

17. Apply finish of choice.

53

Windowpane Bowl

54

Graceful and elegant, the windowpane bowl demonstrates the amazing ability of laminations to hold together even when walls are sanded very thin. I didn't intend for the walls to be quite so thin, but a bad miscut on the very first ring and a reluctance to discard so much good wood let me turn a salvage operation into a really nice bowl. This bowl uses a different sequence of lamination to create a solid top rim. A thin piece of wood that matches the top rim is used for the base to complement the delicacy of the sides.

Materials and Tools

Wood

Bowl:
- (1) 9" x 7" x ¾" (229mm x 178mm x 19mm) maple
- (1) 9" x 7" x ⅛" (229mm x 178mm x 3mm) walnut

Vertical Strips:
- (3) 9" x ¾" x ⅛" (229mm x 19mm x 3mm) walnut

Horizontal Strips:
- (4) 7" x ¾" x ⅛" (178mm x 19mm x 3mm) walnut

Base:
- (1) 7½" x 5½" x ¼" (191mm x 140mm x 6mm) walnut

Materials
- Packing tape (optional)
- Glue
- Repositionable adhesive
- Sanding discs for flexible pad sander, assorted grits 60 to 400
- Sandpaper for inflatable ball sander, assorted grits 60 to 320 (optional)
- Sandpaper for hand sanding, assorted grits 220 to 400
- 0000 steel wool or 320-grit sanding sponge
- Spray shellac or Danish oil

Tools
- Scroll saw blade, size #9
- Drill bit size #54 or ¹⁄₁₆" (2mm)
- Awl
- Ruler
- Bowl press or clamps
- Clamps for lamination
- 2" (51mm) flexible pad sander
- Inflatable ball sander and pump (optional)

Cut the maple lengthwise into strips. Make two copies of the pattern (page 56): one for the lamination and one for cutting the rings. Glue the pattern to the 9" x 7" x ¾" (229mm x 178mm x 19mm) maple with repositionable adhesive and cut the long way into four strips. The center strips will be 1½" (38mm) wide. The side strips will be a little wider; the excess will be cut away later. Number the strips to keep them in order. Sand the sides of the strips smooth.

Glue in the long strips. Insert one 9" (229mm)-long, ¾" (19mm)-wide piece of walnut between each piece of maple and glue them into place. Keep the maple strips in order. Clamp and let dry.

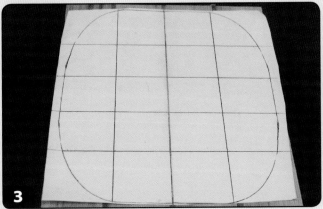

Cut the maple widthwise into strips. Align the centerline of the pattern with the center walnut strip on the blank and attach it with repositionable adhesive. Cut along the four lines that intersect the laminated strips at right angles. Number the strips. Sand the strips as needed so that the three center strips are the same width and all gluing edges are smooth.

Glue in the short strips. Glue in the 7" (178mm) strips a few sections at a time, making sure to keep the strips in order. Let each section set up before adding another one. Clamp and let dry. Sand the top and bottom of the blank smooth.

Glue on the thin piece of walnut. Glue on the piece of 9" x 7" x ⅛" (229mm x 178mm x 3mm) walnut. Clamp and let dry.

Complete the lamination. Sand the laminated blank smooth, if needed. Draw guidelines on the walnut side. Measure the thickness of the blank before cutting and adjust the cutting angle if needed.

Chapter Three: Laminated Wood Bowls

Making the bowl

1. Glue the pattern onto the walnut side of the blank with repositionable adhesive. Be sure the pattern is centered on the guidelines.

2. Tilt the scroll saw table 18°, left side down.

3. Cut the bowl outline in a clockwise direction.

4. Mark the top on the outer rim.

5. Drill the entry hole at an 18° angle and complete the first ring.

6. Mark the top and guidelines on the ring.

7. Use the inside of each ring to mark the outline for the next ring.

8. Cut two additional rings.

9. Stack the rings and check for spaces between them.

10. Glue the rings, clamp them, and let dry.

11. Sand the inside of the bowl smooth.

12. Trace the outline of the bottom ring onto the ¼" (6mm) piece of walnut.

13. Cut along the traced line at an 18° angle, left side down, cutting clockwise.

14. Glue on the base, clamp, and let dry.

15. Sand the outside and upper edge of the bowl.

16. Apply finish of choice.

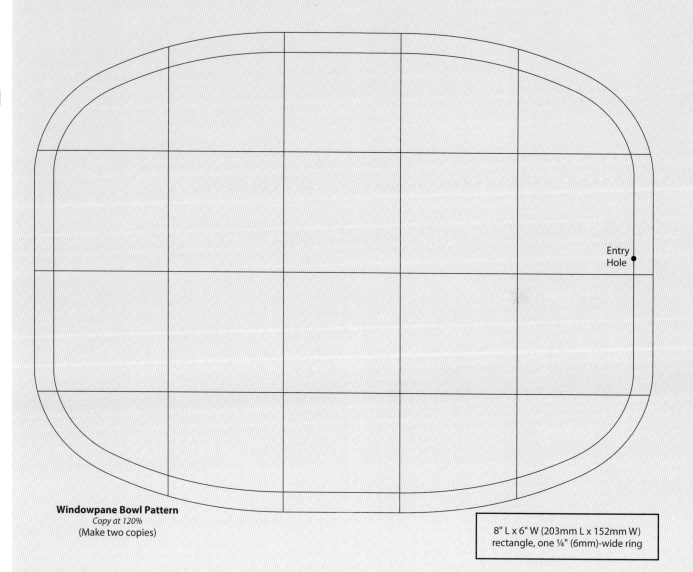

Entry Hole

Windowpane Bowl Pattern
Copy at 120%
(Make two copies)

8" L x 6" W (203mm L x 152mm W) rectangle, one ¼" (6mm)-wide ring

Triple-Swirl Bowl

Here is a perfect use for those pieces of wood too small for most purposes but too good to discard. For the most attractive bowl, choose pieces of wood that contrast with each other. Note that the patterns indicate the direction of the grain for each piece. This is done to maximize the amount of face grain, which is usually more attractive than end grain, that will show on the sides of the bowl. Stagger the rings as much or as little as you like when gluing up the bowl.

Materials and Tools

Wood
* (1) 4" x 7" x ¾" (102mm x 178mm x 19mm) cherry
* (1) 4" x 7" x ¾" (102mm x 178mm x 19mm) maple
* (1) 4" x 7" x ¾" (102mm x 178mm x 19mm) teak

Materials
* Packing tape (optional)
* Glue
* Repositionable adhesive
* Rubber band (for clamping the lamination)
* Sanding discs for flexible pad sander, assorted grits 60 to 400
* Sandpaper for inflatable ball sander, assorted grits 60 to 320 (optional)

* Sandpaper for hand sanding, assorted grits 220 to 400
* 0000 steel wool or 320-grit sanding sponge
* Spray shellac or Danish oil

Tools
* Scroll saw blade, size #9
* Drill bit size #54 or ¹⁄₁₆" (2mm)
* Awl
* Bowl press or clamps
* 2" (51mm) flexible pad sander
* Inflatable ball sander and pump (optional)

Lamination guide

1. Make two copies of the pattern. Cut one in pieces for the lamination and use the other as a cutting guide.

2. Glue the pattern to each piece of wood with repositionable adhesive. Be sure to orient the grain in the direction of the arrow.

3. Cut slightly to the outside of the straight cut lines. This will let you sand the sides to achieve a good fit for gluing. Cut generously to the outside of the curved cut line so that when you glue up the pieces your blank will be a little larger than the pattern. This will make it easier to cut the first ring..

4. Test the fit of the segments, and sand the sides as needed until the segments fit together tightly.

5. Glue the segments together. Clamp them with a rubber band and let dry.

6. Sand the blank smooth.

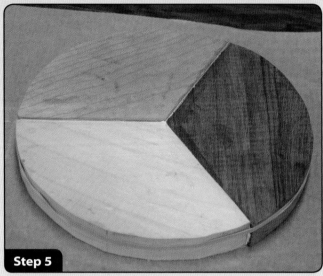

Step 5

Glue the three segments together.

Alternate version

To make the alternate version of this bowl, you will need to make the following changes to the materials and instructions:

- Top rim is less sharply contoured

- Ginger jar base (page 112) is used

Making the bowl

1. Glue the pattern to the laminated blank with repositionable adhesive, using an awl to center the pattern.

2. Drill entry holes at a 28° angle.

3. Cut the outside of the first ring at a 28° angle, left side down, cutting clockwise.

4. Mark the top of the outer rim.

5. Insert the blade through the first entry hole and complete the first ring.

6. Cut two additional rings in the same manner, marking the top of each ring.

7. Stack the rings so that the laminated pieces are staggered.

8. Check for spaces between the rings.

9. Glue the rings, clamp them, and let dry.

10. Sand the inside of the bowl smooth.

11. Glue on the base, staggering the lamination. Clamp and let dry.

12. Sand the outside and upper edge of the bowl.

13. Apply finish of choice.

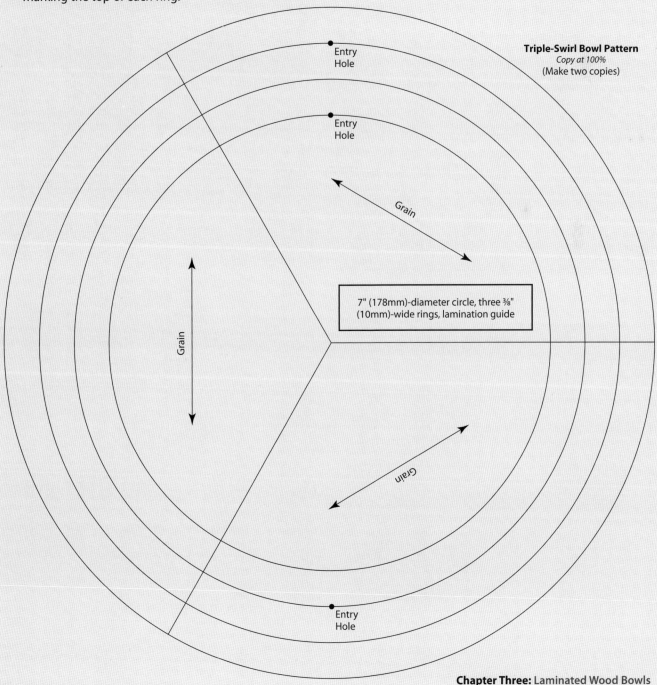

Entry Hole

Entry Hole

Triple-Swirl Bowl Pattern
Copy at 100%
(Make two copies)

Grain

Grain

Grain

7" (178mm)-diameter circle, three ⅜" (10mm)-wide rings, lamination guide

Entry Hole

4

Multiple-Angle Bowls

The bowls in this chapter, like those in previous chapters, are made from a single piece of wood, either plain or laminated, that is cut into concentric rings. They differ from the earlier bowls in that some rings for each project are cut at a different angle from the rest, and some rings may be re-cut for additional shaping. This selective variation of the angle allows for subtle or dramatic changes in the shape of the sides, bottoms, and top rims, and provides more options than possible with sanding alone.

These projects incorporate multiple cutting angles, which allow for more drastic changes in the shapes of the bowls.

Combining dark teak and light maple creates a striking yet easy-to-make bowl. The bowl blank is laminated in several steps to produce a crisscross look. To achieve the effect of a separate base, the lower edge of the glued-up rings and upper edge of the base are contoured separately before being glued together. This unusual effect was created by accident when I rounded the lower edge of the glued-up rings by mistake and needed to figure out some way to save the bowl.

Materials and Tools

Wood
- (1) 9" x 8" x ¾" (229mm x 203mm x 19mm) teak
- (2) 12" x 1¼" x ¾" (305mm x 32mm x 19mm) maple

Materials
- Packing tape (optional)
- Glue
- Repositionable adhesive
- Sanding discs for flexible pad sander, assorted grits 60 to 400
- Sandpaper for inflatable ball sander, assorted grits 60 to 320 (optional)
- Sandpaper for hand sanding, assorted grits 220 to 400
- 0000 steel wool or 320-grit sanding sponge
- Spray shellac or Danish oil

Tools
- Scroll saw blade, size #9
- Drill bit size #54 or ⅟₁₆" (2mm)
- Awl
- Ruler
- Bowl press or clamps
- Clamps for lamination
- 2" (51mm) flexible pad sander
- Inflatable ball sander and pump (optional)

1

Insert the first maple strip. Make two copies of the pattern (page 67): one for the lamination and the other for cutting the rings. Cut the teak diagonally from point to point. Insert one of the maple strips, keeping the grain of the teak aligned. Glue, clamp, and let dry.

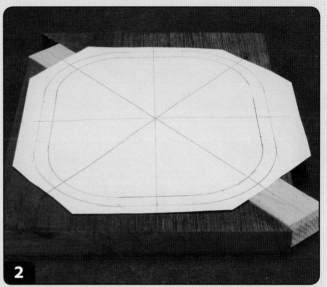

2

Make the second cut. Draw a line down the center of the maple strip. Align the pattern with that line and attach with repositionable adhesive. Use the pattern to mark the ends of the second diagonal. Draw the second diagonal on the wood and cut along that line.

3

Complete the lamination. Insert the second piece of maple between the cut edges of the teak, keeping the grain of the teak aligned. Glue, clamp, and let dry. Trim off the protruding edges, if desired, to make blank easier to handle.

Gluing on the diagonal

Gluing up wood cut on the diagonal can be tricky. Glue that sets up quickly with a good "grab," such as Weldbond, makes the process easier. If you rub the glued pieces together to force out air bubbles and let them set up for a minute or two, they will be less likely to slide when you apply the clamp. If you still get slippage, remove the clamp, slide the pieces carefully back into position without breaking the seal, and let them dry without clamping. If the pieces mated properly, the clamping that was done should be sufficient to obtain a good join.

Making the bowl

1

Drawing the guidelines. Using the crossed maple pieces as a guide, draw intersecting guidelines on the bowl blank.

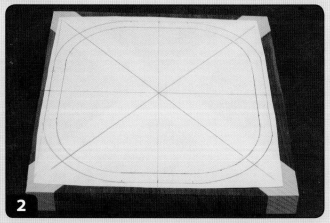

2

Gluing the pattern. Apply repositionable adhesive to the pattern. Push the point of an awl through the center of the pattern and place the point on the center of the bowl blank. Align the pattern with the guidelines drawn on the wood.

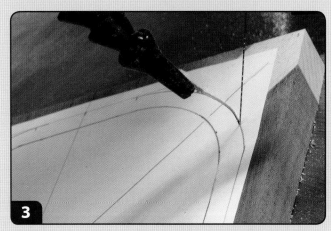

3

Cutting the outline. Tilt saw table to 30°, left side down. Cut clockwise along the outer line.

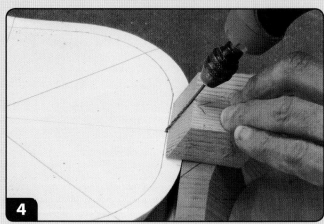

4

Drilling the entry hole for the first ring. Using a tilting drill press or 30° angle guide, drill an entry hole on the inner circle at 30°, angled toward the center of the blank.

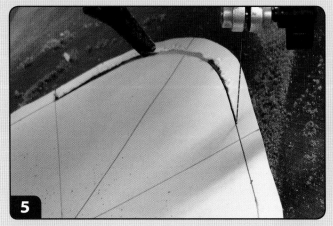

5

Completing the first ring. Insert the blade through the entry hole and cut clockwise along the line to complete the first ring.

6

Marking the first ring. Place the ring on the blank, mark the top, and transfer the guidelines from the blank. The blank may be slightly larger than the ring because of the steeper cutting angle. This will be sanded smooth when you shape the outside of the bowl.

7

Outlining the second ring. Keeping the first ring in place on the blank, trace the inside of the first ring. This is the cutting line for the second ring.

8

Drilling the entry hole for the second ring. Drill a 28° entry hole on the second ring, using an angle guide or a tilting drill press. This change in angle gives a gentle flare to the top ring.

9

Cutting the second ring. Tilt the scroll saw table to 28°, left side down. Insert the blade through the entry hole and cut clockwise on the marked line.

10

Marking the second ring and tracing outline for third ring. Place the second ring on the blank, mark the top, and transfer the guidelines. Trace the inside of the second ring to form the outline for the third ring.

11

Cutting the third ring. Drill a 28° entry hole and cut the third ring at a 28° angle. The remaining piece will become the base.

12

Cutting the base. Tilt the saw table 35°, left side down. Using the top edge of the base as a guide, cut around the base clockwise. Do not cut into the top of the base. The purpose of this cut is to increase the angle of the base.

Making the bowl *(continued)*

13

Preparing the rings. Stack the three rings and check for spaces. Sand if necessary. Transfer all marks to the outer and inner edges and erase all marks from the top surface of the lower rings.

14

Gluing the rings. Glue the three rings together, keeping the maple stripes aligned. Clamp the rings and let them dry.

15

Sanding the rings. Sand the inner and outer faces of the rings until they are smooth, using the inflatable ball and flexible pad sanders.

16

Shaping the top ring. Accentuate the flare in the top ring using the flexible pad sander.

17

Shaping the bottom ring. Sand the lower edge into a curved shape.

18

Shaping the base. Using the flexible pad sander, contour the upper edge of the base into a curved shape to match the lower edge of the rings. Sand the entire base smooth.

19

Gluing on the base. Glue the base to the ring assembly. Clamp the bowl and let dry.

20

Finishing the bowl. Apply mineral spirits to the bowl to reveal any glue spots. Mark them with a white pencil or chalk. When the bowl is dry, sand off the glue spots. Apply the first coat of shellac and let dry. Smooth the surface with a 320-grit sanding sponge or 0000 steel wool. Vacuum, remove any remaining particles with a damp cloth or paper towel, and recoat. Repeat until the desired finish is obtained.

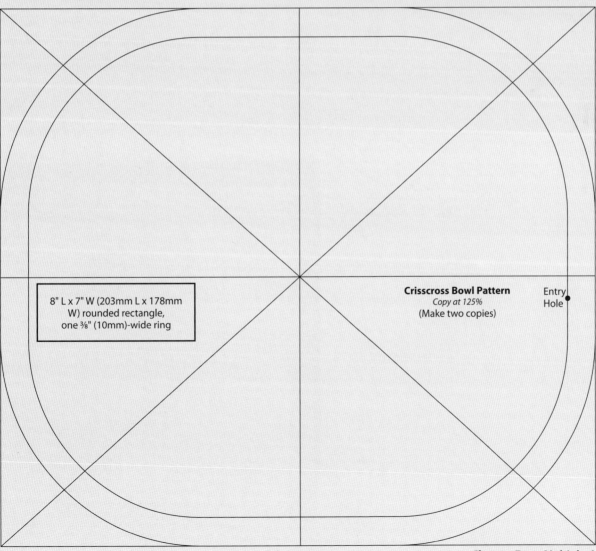

8" L x 7" W (203mm L x 178mm W) rounded rectangle, one ⅜" (10mm)-wide ring

Crisscross Bowl Pattern
Copy at 125%
(Make two copies)

Entry Hole

Flared Five-Lobed Bowl

This five-lobed bowl is the perfect showcase for a full-flared upper rim. A three-step cutting process is used to create the flare on the first ring. The first two cuts produce a ring with a steep outside angle and a moderate inside angle. The third cut is a waste removal cut made on the inside of the ring. This cut makes shaping the flare more controllable and reduces the amount of sanding needed. I used a piece of hickory from the "cut-off" pile for this bowl, and found that while its hardness made it a challenge to shape, the beauty of the grain made the extra work worthwhile.

Materials and Tools

Wood
- (1) 8" x 8" x ¾" (203mm x 203mm x 19mm) hickory, or wood of choice

Materials
- Packing tape (optional)
- Glue
- Repositionable adhesive
- Sanding discs for flexible pad sander, assorted grits 60 to 400
- Sandpaper for inflatable ball sander, assorted grits 60 to 320 (optional)
- Sandpaper for hand sanding, assorted grits 220 to 400

- 0000 steel wool or 320-grit sanding pad
- Spray shellac or Danish oil

Tools
- Scroll saw blade, size #9
- Drill bit size #54 or ¹⁄₁₆" (2mm)
- Awl
- Ruler
- Bowl press or clamps
- 2" (51mm) flexible pad sander
- Inflatable ball sander and pump (optional)

Making the bowl

1. Draw guidelines on the bowl blank. Use the awl to align the pattern with the guidelines. Glue on the pattern with repositionable adhesive.

2. Cut the outline at a 40° angle, saw table left side down, cutting clockwise.

3. Drill a 25° entry hole on the inner line. Tilt the saw table at a 25° angle, left side down, and cut clockwise to complete the first ring. Your ring will be about ⅜" (10mm) wide at the bottom edge. Remove the pattern.

4. Make a 40° waste removal cut in the first ring, about ⅜" (10mm) from the outer edge. Do not cut into the lower edge of the ring.

5. Place the first ring on the blank. Mark the top and transfer the guidelines to the sides of the ring. Trace the inner profile of the first ring on the blank to form the cutting line for the second ring.

6. Drill an entry hole at a 28° angle. Cut out the second ring at a 28° angle, table tilted left side down, cutting clockwise. Mark the top and transfer the guidelines.

7. Stack the rings, align them, and check for spaces.

8. Glue up the rings. Clamp and let dry.

9. Sand the inside of the bowl smooth.

10. Glue on the base. Clamp and let dry.

11. Sand and shape the outside of the bowl and the flared upper edge.

12. Apply finish of choice.

Waste removal cuts

Waste removal cuts are used to create top rings with a pronounced outward flare. The outer circle of the top ring is cut at a designated steep angle and the inner circle is cut at a less extreme angle. This results in a ring that is narrower on the bottom face than on the top. A secondary cut is made on the inner ring to accentuate the flare while leaving the base of the ring intact.

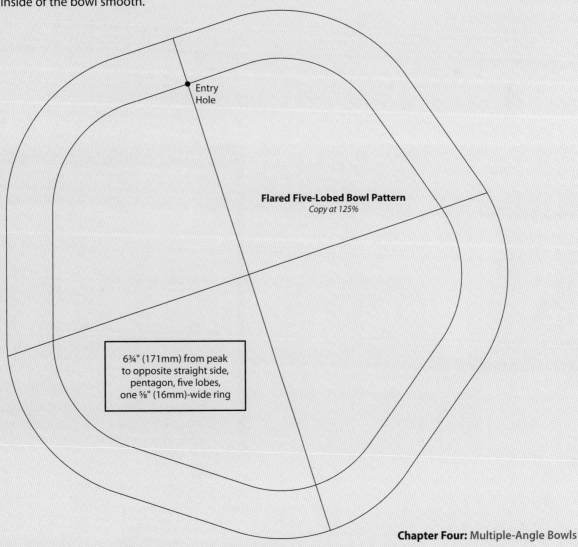

Entry Hole

Flared Five-Lobed Bowl Pattern
Copy at 125%

6¾" (171mm) from peak to opposite straight side, pentagon, five lobes, one ⅝" (16mm)-wide ring

Ripple-Edged Round Bowl

This dainty round bowl features a rim with ten petal-like flutes. What differentiates this bowl from other petal-shaped bowls in this book is that only the top rim is petal shaped; the rest of the bowl is round. The top shaping is done after the rings are cut. This technique allows you to put a decorative edge on a bowl or vase of any appropriate shape (see Ripple-Edged Vase, page 126). Since the bowl is a small one, the base will be more in proportion if its thickness is reduced slightly by sanding its lower face with a disc or belt sander before it is glued to the rings.

Materials and Tools

Wood
- (1) 7½" x 7½" x ¾" (191mm x 191mm x 19mm) mahogany

Materials
- Packing tape (optional)
- Glue
- Repositionable adhesive
- Sanding discs for flexible pad sander, assorted grits 60 to 400
- Sandpaper for inflatable ball sander, assorted grits 60 to 320 (optional)
- Sandpaper for hand sanding, assorted grits 220 to 400
- 0000 steel wool or 320-grit sanding sponge
- Spray shellac or Danish oil

Tools
- Scroll saw blade, size #9
- Drill bit size #54 or ¹⁄₁₆" (2mm)
- Awl
- Ruler
- Bowl press or clamps
- 2" (51mm) flexible pad sander
- Inflatable ball sander and pump (optional)

Making the bowl

1. Draw guidelines on the bowl blank.

2. Glue the bowl pattern to the blank with repositionable adhesive, using the awl to align the guidelines.

3. Cut the outer circle clockwise at a 30° angle, saw table tilted left side down.

4. Drill an entry hole on the inner circle at 20°.

5. Cut the inner circle at a 20° angle, saw table tilted left side down, cutting clockwise. Remove pattern.

6. Place the completed first ring on the bowl blank. Don't worry if the edge hangs over a bit; it will be sanded smooth when you sand the outside of the bowl. Mark the top and transfer the guidelines.

7. Trace the inner circle to form a cutting line for the second ring.

8. Drill a 20° entry hole for the second ring.

9. Cut the second ring at 20°.

10. Bevel the remaining piece (the base) to 30°, using the upper profile as a guide (see sidebar, Beveling the base, page 72).

11. Glue the petal-shaped pattern (page 72) to the top ring with repositionable adhesive and follow the instructions to create a scalloped edge (see sidebar, Cutting a petal edge on a round bowl, page 73). The ring will look rough after the preliminary sanding. The sanding will be completed after the bowl is glued up.

12. Glue the rings together, clamp, and let dry.

13. Sand the inside of the rings smooth, keeping the inside of the bottom ring round.

14. If desired, reduce the thickness of the base by sanding the underside.

15. Glue the base to the rings, clamp, and let dry.

16. Finish shaping the petals, using the inflatable ball and flexible pad sanders.

17. Sand the outside of the bowl smooth.

18. Apply finish of choice.

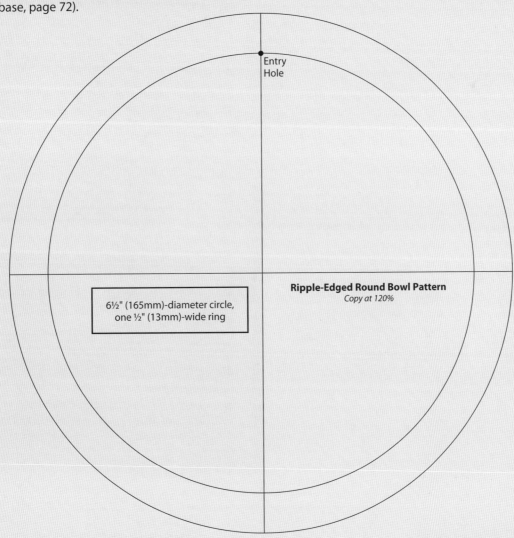

Entry
Hole

Ripple-Edged Round Bowl Pattern
Copy at 120%

6½" (165mm)-diameter circle,
one ½" (13mm)-wide ring

**Ripple-Edged Round Bowl
Edge Cutting Guide Pattern**
Copy at 100%

Eight ripple cutting guide,
6½" (165mm)-diameter circle,
one ½" (13mm)-wide ring

Beveling the base

To cut down on the amount of sanding needed to contour the base, excess wood can be removed by using the top profile of the base as a guide to give the base a steeper angle. Once the excess wood is removed, the base is sanded as usual to complete the shaping.

Cutting a petal edge on a round bowl

To get a petal effect on a round bowl, the petals must be cut into the top ring after it has been cut to maintain the roundness of the lower edge. To do this, cuts are made into the inner and outer edges of the ring at angles that do not interfere with the shape of the lower edge. Here's how:

Attaching the pattern. Glue the pattern for the petal edge to the top rim with repositionable adhesive.

Cutting the outer petals. Tilt the scroll saw table 15°, left side down. Cut clockwise along the outer edge of the pattern.

Cutting the inner petals. Tilt the saw table 40°, left side down. Cut clockwise along the inner edge of the pattern. Be careful not to cut into the lower edge of the ring.

Sanding the outside. Smooth the outer edge with a spindle sander, table set to 15°.

Sanding the inside. Smooth the inner edge with a spindle sander, table set to 40°.

Completing the rough-sanding. The ring is left rough at this point to avoid damage during glue-up. Final sanding will be done after the bowl is glued together.

Four-Petal Curved Bowl

This gently curved bowl is a variation of the petal bowl, but is somewhat less demanding to cut and shape because of its fewer lobes and wider inner curves. Simple in design, it is ideally suited for wood with an interesting color or grain. For ease in sanding, place entry holes on curved areas, not at points.

Materials and Tools

Wood
- (1) 8" x 8" x ¾" (203mm x 203mm x 19mm) cherry

Materials
- Packing tape (optional)
- Glue
- Repositionable adhesive
- Sanding discs for flexible pad sander, assorted grits 60 to 400
- Sandpaper for inflatable ball sander, assorted grits 60 to 320 (optional)
- Sandpaper for hand sanding, assorted grits 220 to 400

- 0000 steel wool or 320-grit sanding sponge
- Spray shellac or Danish oil

Tools
- Scroll saw blade, size #9
- Drill bit size #54 or ⅟₁₆" (2mm)
- Awl
- Ruler
- Bowl press or clamps
- 2" (51mm) flexible pad sander
- Inflatable ball sander and pump (optional)

Making the bowl

1. Draw guidelines on the bowl blank.

2. Glue on the pattern with repositionable adhesive, using the awl to center it on the blank.

3. Tilt the scroll saw table to 20°, left side down. Cut clockwise along the outer line.

4. Drill a 20° entry hole on the inner line and cut to complete first ring. Remove pattern.

5. Place the ring on the blank. Mark the top and transfer the guidelines from the blank.

6. Trace the inside of the first ring to form the cutting line for the second ring.

7. Drill a 25° entry hole on the second ring and cut clockwise with the saw table tilted 25°, left side down.

8. Place the second ring on the blank, mark the top, and transfer the guidelines. Trace the inside of the second ring to form the cutting line for the third ring.

9. Drill a 35° entry hole and cut the third ring clockwise, table tilted 35°, left side down.

10. Glue up the rings, clamp, and let dry.

11. Sand the inside of the rings smooth.

12. Glue on the base, clamp, and let dry.

13. Contour the base to obtain a nicely rounded shape.

14. Sand the outside of the bowl smooth.

15. Apply finish of choice.

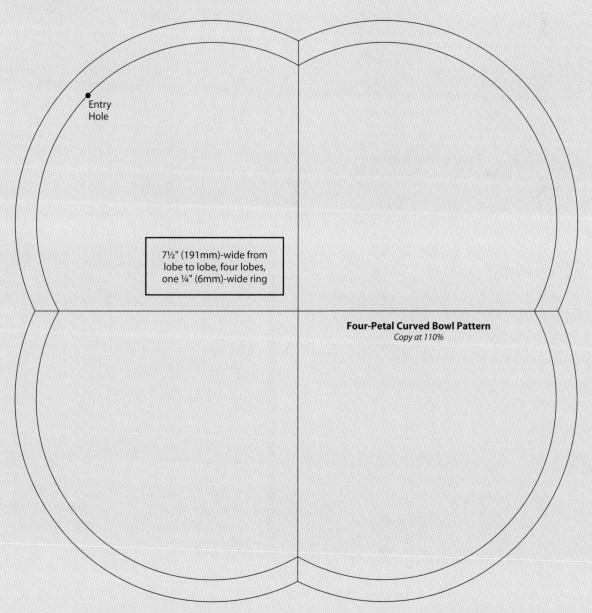

Entry Hole

7½" (191mm)-wide from lobe to lobe, four lobes, one ¼" (6mm)-wide ring

Four-Petal Curved Bowl Pattern
Copy at 110%

Heart-Shaped Bowl

This delicate curved bowl is the perfect gift for an engagement or anniversary. I used a light-colored piece of poplar with a pretty grain, but most any wood should work. To facilitate sanding, place entry holes on flat or curved surfaces only, not at top or bottom points. Once glued up, the bottom can be sanded aggressively to create a nicely curved shape, but check carefully as you sand to keep the bowl symmetrical.

Materials and Tools

Wood
❖ (1) 8" x 8" x ¾" (203mm x 203mm x 19mm) poplar

Materials
❖ Packing tape (optional)
❖ Glue
❖ Repositionable adhesive
❖ Sanding discs for flexible pad sander, assorted grits 60 to 400
❖ Sandpaper for inflatable ball sander, assorted grits 60 to 320 (optional)
❖ Sandpaper for hand sanding, assorted grits 220 to 400

❖ 0000 steel wool or 320-grit sanding sponge
❖ Spray shellac or Danish oil

Tools
❖ Scroll saw blade, size #9
❖ Drill bit size #54 or ¹⁄₁₆" (2mm)
❖ Awl
❖ Ruler
❖ Bowl press or clamps
❖ 2" (51mm) flexible pad sander
❖ Inflatable ball sander and pump (optional)

Making the bowl

1. Draw guidelines on the bowl blank.

2. Glue the pattern to the wood with repositionable adhesive, aligning the guidelines.

3. Cut the outline at 20°, saw table tilted left side down, cutting clockwise.

4. Drill an entry hole on the inside of the first ring at 20° and complete the cutting of the first ring. Remove the pattern.

5. Place the first ring on the bowl blank.

6. Transfer the guidelines and trace the outline for second ring.

7. Drill an entry hole at 25° for the second ring.

8. Cut the ring at 25°, saw table left side down, cutting clockwise.

9. Place the second ring on the bowl blank and transfer the guidelines.

10. Trace the outline for the third ring.

11. Drill an entry hole at 35° for the third ring.

12. Cut the ring at 35°, saw table left side down, cutting clockwise.

13. Glue the rings together, clamp, and let dry.

14. Sand the inside of the rings smooth.

15. Glue on the base, clamp the bowl, and let it dry.

16. Contour the base as desired.

17. Sand the outside of the bowl smooth.

18. Apply finish of choice.

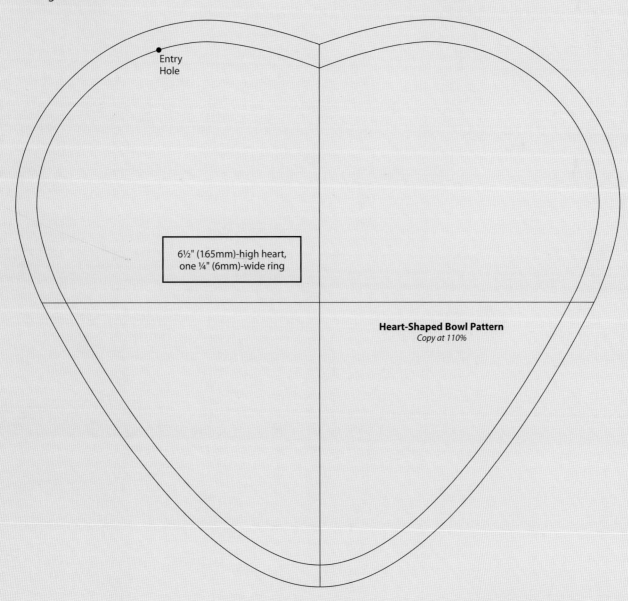

Entry
Hole

6½" (165mm)-high heart,
one ¼" (6mm)-wide ring

Heart-Shaped Bowl Pattern
Copy at 110%

5

Thin Wood Bowls

Graceful, delicate bowls can be crafted from thinner stock. This chapter features bowls made from wood that is less than ¾" (19mm) thick. The construction principles are the same as for bowls made from thicker wood, but a steeper cutting angle is required for the same ring width. Thin wood bowls are a natural for colorful laminations, or for showcasing beautifully grained pieces of wood that might be too challenging to use as thicker stock.

Bowls created from thin stock—less than ¾" (19mm)—require a steeper cutting angle.

This multi-segment bowl is made from thin pieces of purpleheart and mahogany, although any two contrasting woods will work. The lamination is somewhat time consuming, but once completed, the bowl cuts quickly and easily, and looks as though you spent many hours gluing scores of pieces together. Two easy-to-make jigs help the task go more smoothly. The semi-circle construction method lets you use narrow pieces of stock, which you are likely to have on hand as leftovers from other projects.

Materials and Tools

Wood

❖ (2) 8" x 4" x ¼" (203mm x 102mm x 6mm) purpleheart
❖ (2) 8" x 4" x ¼" (203mm x 102mm x 6mm) mahogany
❖ Scrap of ¼" (6mm) purpleheart (optional)

Materials

❖ Packing tape (optional)
❖ Double-sided tape
❖ Glue
❖ Repositionable adhesive
❖ Sanding discs for flexible pad sander, assorted grits 60 to 400
❖ Sandpaper for inflatable ball sander, assorted grits 60 to 320 (optional)
❖ Sandpaper for hand sanding, assorted grits 220 to 400

❖ 0000 steel wool or 320-grit sanding sponge
❖ Spray shellac or Danish oil

Tools

❖ Scroll saw blade, size #9
❖ Drill bit size #54 or ¹⁄₁₆" (2mm)
❖ Awl
❖ Ruler
❖ Compass
❖ Bowl press or clamps
❖ Clamps for lamination
❖ 2" (51mm) flexible pad sander
❖ Inflatable ball sander and pump (optional)
❖ ½" (13mm) drill bit and ½" (13mm) plug cutter (optional)
❖ Gluing jig (recommended)
❖ Alignment jig (recommended)

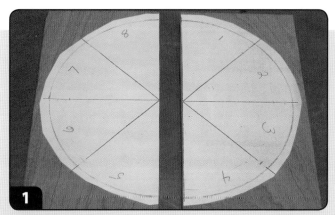

1

Prepare the wood. Attach one piece of mahogany to one piece of purpleheart with double-sided tape. Place the tape so that the pieces will hold together after the circle is cut. Repeat for the other pieces of mahogany and purpleheart. Cut the lamination guide in half and glue one half to each piece of taped wood with repositionable adhesive.

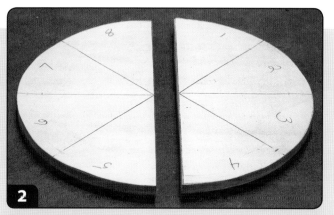

2

Cut the perimeter. Cut out the perimeter of the pattern for each piece.

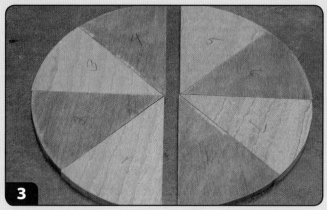

3

Cut the segments. Cut along the lines to divide each piece into four segments. Remove the pattern from each segment. Separate the segments and write the number from the pattern on both top and bottom pieces. Assemble segments to make four semicircles, alternating colors and keeping the numbers in order.

4

Glue the semicircles. Glue up each semicircle using the alignment jig (see sidebar on page 82). Place waxed paper between the wood and the jig to prevent sticking. Use finger pressure to clamp the segments together. Press the segments against the strip of wood to get a flat edge. Let dry.

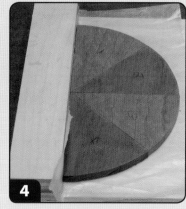

5

Complete the circles. Glue each semicircle to its mating half to form two complete circles. You may need to sand the straight edges before gluing if they are not perfectly flat. Be sure the numbers on the wedges go in order for each circle. Clamp each circle in the gluing jig (see sidebar on page 82) to get a good join. Let dry.

6

Complete the lamination. Stack the circles so that the numbers on the top and bottom segments are the same and the colors alternate. Make an alignment mark on the outside edge so you can reposition the pieces properly when gluing up. Erase all other marks and sand all faces smooth. Place one circle on waxed paper on the plywood circle from the gluing jig. Spread glue evenly over the surface. Place the other circle on top, using the mark on the edge to align it properly. Cover with waxed paper, clamp tightly, and let dry overnight. Bowl press shown on its side for illustrative purposes.

81

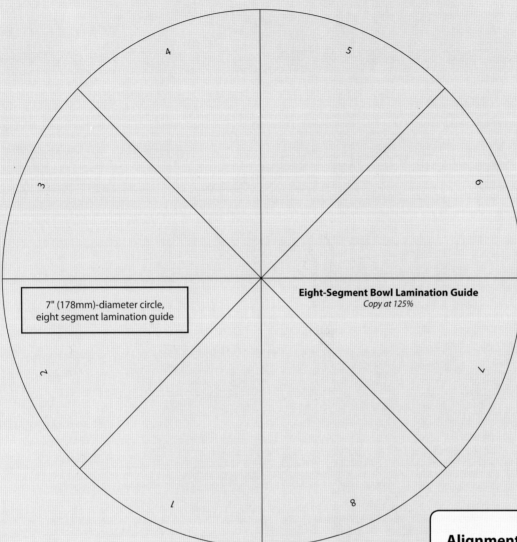

4   5

3   6

2   7

1   8

7" (178mm)-diameter circle,
eight segment lamination guide

Eight-Segment Bowl Lamination Guide
Copy at 125%

Alignment jig

Materials
❖ (1) 8½" x 8½" x ½" (216mm
   x 216mm x 13mm) plywood
❖ (1) 8½" x 1½" x ¾" (216mm
   x 38mm x 19mm) plywood
   or hardwood

This quickly made jig provides support
for the segments as you glue up the
semicircles. To make the jig, glue the
hardwood strip to the edge of the
plywood. Clamp and let dry.

Gluing jig

Materials
❖ (1) 12" x 7½" x ¾" (305mm x 191mm x 19mm) plywood

This simple jig makes it easier to
clamp the semicircles when you
glue them to each other. Cut a
7½" (191mm) circle out of the
center of the plywood. Use the
sidepieces to apply clamping
pressure to the semicircles when
you glue them together, and the
center circle for extra height in
the bowl press.

1

Marking the first ring. Draw two intersecting guidelines on the bowl blank. Place the point of your compass in the center and draw a circle that is 6½" (165mm) in diameter. This is the outer cutting line for the first ring. Make a mark on a guideline that is ⅜" (10mm) inside that circle. Use your compass to draw a smaller circle that forms the inside edge of the first ring.

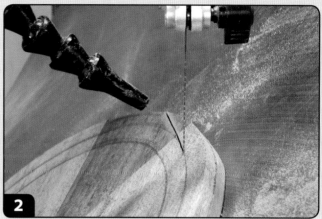

2

Cutting the outer profile. Tilt the saw table 38°, left side down. Cut clockwise along the outer circle. Mark the top.

3

Drilling the first entry hole. Drill an entry hole on the inner ring at a 38° angle using an angle guide or a drill press with a tilting table.

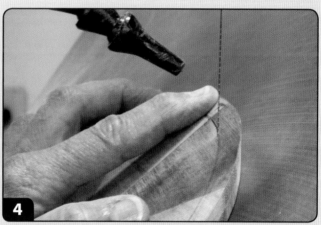

4

Completing the first ring. Insert the blade into the entry hole and cut along the inner line to complete the first ring. Mark the top.

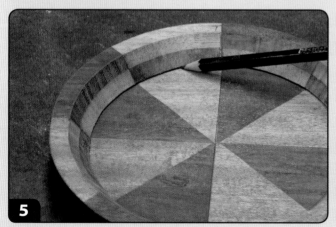

5

Marking the second ring. Place the first ring on the bowl blank, aligning the tops, and trace the inside of the first ring on the blank. This is the cutting line for the second ring. You do not need to make additional marks since the lamination pattern will guide the alignment when gluing the bowl together.

6

Drilling the second ring entry hole. Drill an entry hole for the second ring on the opposite side from the first entry hole. Avoid placing entry holes back to back on the same ring.

Chapter Five: Thin Wood Bowls

83

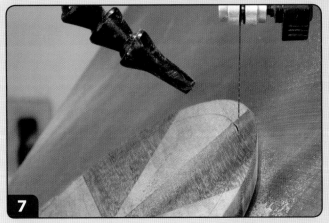

7

Cutting the second ring. Insert the blade in the second entry hole and cut out the second ring. Mark the top.

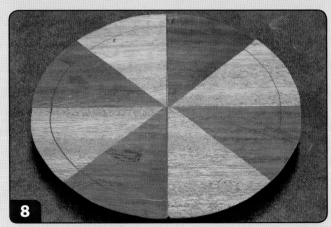

8

Marking the third ring. Place the second ring on the bowl blank, aligning the tops. Trace the inside of the second ring on the bowl blank. This is the cutting line for the third ring.

9

Cutting the third ring. Drill an entry hole for the third ring, cut and mark as for the second ring.

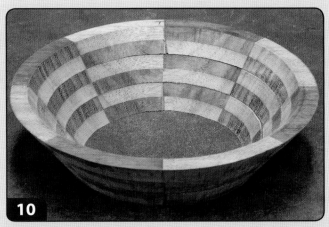

10

Stacking and checking for spaces. Stack the rings, aligning the tops. Check for spaces between the rings and sand if necessary. Remove any pencil marks from the face of the rings.

11

Gluing the rings. Glue up the rings, aligning the top marks and laminations, and clamp. Do not glue on the base at this time. If using the bowl press, do not over-tighten, since this could distort the laminated rings. Remove the bowl after a few minutes and clean off excess glue. Reclamp the bowl and let dry.

12

Sanding the inside of the bowl. Sand the inside of the bowl smooth using a spindle sander, flexible sanding pad, or inflatable sanding ball. Work from coarser to finer grits.

13

Inserting a plug in the base. This is an optional step. If the segments don't meet evenly in the center, or if you want a more decorative effect, cut a ½" (13mm)-diameter plug of purpleheart from a scrap of ¼" (6mm) stock. Drill a ½" (13mm)-diameter hole in the center of the bowl base, slightly less than ¼" (6mm)-deep and glue the plug into place. Sand flush.

14

Gluing on the base. Glue on the base, keeping the top aligned with the rings. If you've used the plug, be sure it is centered. Clamp glued up bowl and let dry.

15

Sanding the outside and contouring. Sand the outside of the bowl smooth, working from coarser to finer grits. Contour the upper and lower edges.

16

Finishing the bowl. Apply mineral spirits to the bowl to reveal any glue spots. Mark them with a white pencil or chalk. When dry, sand off the glue spots. Apply the first coat of shellac and let dry. Smooth the surface with a 320-grit sanding sponge or 0000 steel wool. Vacuum, remove any remaining particles with a damp cloth or paper towel, and then recoat. Repeat until the desired finish is obtained.

Alternate version

To make the alternate version of this bowl, you will need to make the following changes to the materials and instructions:

- Materials and bowl size are the same

- Ring width is ¼" (6mm) instead of ⅜" (10mm)

- Cutting angle is 28° instead of 38°

- Five rings are cut instead of three

This colorful bowl is made from two circles, each containing twenty segments. Like the Eight-Segment Bowl (page 80), it is formed from semicircles glued together to form full circles. However, to produce a swirl effect these circles are rotated when glued together.

The use of so many little pieces poses both organizational and gluing challenges. Numbering each segment when removing the pattern easily solves the organizational challenge. The gluing challenge is solved by use of an alignment jig (see sidebar on page 82) to keep them in place.

Materials and Tools

Wood
- ❖ (2) 8" x 4" x ¼" (203mm x 102mm x 6mm) purpleheart
- ❖ (2) 8" x 4" x ¼" (203mm x 102mm x 6mm) yellowheart
- ❖ Scrap of ½" (13mm) purpleheart for center plug

Materials
- ❖ Packing tape (optional)
- ❖ Glue
- ❖ Repositionable adhesive
- ❖ Double-sided tape
- ❖ Sanding discs for flexible pad sander, assorted grits 60 to 400
- ❖ Sandpaper for inflatable ball sander, assorted grits 60 to 320 (optional)
- ❖ Sandpaper for hand sanding, assorted grits 220 to 400
- ❖ 0000 steel wool or 320-grit sanding sponge
- ❖ Spray shellac or Danish oil

Tools
- ❖ Scroll saw blade, size #9
- ❖ Drill bit size #54 or ¹⁄₁₆" (2mm)
- ❖ Awl
- ❖ Ruler
- ❖ Compass
- ❖ Bowl press or clamps
- ❖ Clamps for lamination
- ❖ 2" (51mm) flexible pad sander
- ❖ Inflatable ball sander and pump (optional)
- ❖ ½" (13mm) drill bit and ½" (13mm) plug cutter
- ❖ Gluing jig (recommended, see page 82)
- ❖ Alignment jig (recommended, see page 82)

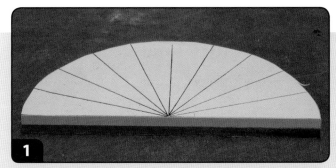

1

Prepare the wood. Attach one piece of yellowheart and one piece of purpleheart with double-sided tape. Place the tape so that the pieces will hold together after the outer circle is cut. Repeat for the other pieces of yellowheart and purpleheart. Cut a lamination guide pattern (page 88) in half and glue one half to each piece of taped wood with repositionable adhesive. Cut along the curved line for each piece to form a semicircle.

2

Number the segments. Number the segments 1–10 on the first piece, 11–20 on the second piece.

3

Cut the segments. Cut along the lines to divide each piece into ten segments. Separate the matching pieces and number each lower piece the same as its matching upper piece. Assemble the pieces to make four semicircles. The pieces should align easily. However, if you are having trouble obtaining a tight fit because the ends of some of the segments are too long and won't lie flat, sand a little off those ends. Although this will result in a small space in the center, the plug that is inserted later will ensure a finished look.

4

Glue up the semicircles. Glue up each semicircle using the gluing jig. Place waxed paper underneath to prevent wood from sticking to the jig. Press the pieces together firmly, then let dry. No clamping is necessary.

6

Glue the circles together. Stack the circles so that the numbers on the top and bottom segments match. Rotate the top circle half a segment. Draw an alignment mark on the outside edge. Erase all other pencil marks and sand the faces smooth. Place waxed paper on the plywood circle from the gluing jig. Place one circle on top. Spread glue evenly over the surface. Place the other circle on top, matching alignment marks. Cover with waxed paper, clamp, and let dry overnight.

5

Glue the semicircles together. Glue each semicircle to its matching half to form two complete circles. Be sure the numbers on the wedges go in order for each circle. Use the gluing jig to get a good join, and let dry.

Chapter Five: Thin Wood Bowls

87

Multi-Colored Twenty Segment Bowl

Making the bowl

1. Draw guidelines on the blank.

2. Attach the cutting pattern (page 89) to the blank with repositionable adhesive. Use the awl to center the pattern on the lamination.

3. Tilt the saw table 28°, left side down.

4. Cut along the bowl outline, cutting clockwise. Mark the top on the outer rim.

5. Drill 28° entry holes, alternating sides, and cut out five rings.

6. Mark the top of each ring.

7. Stack the rings, rotating every other ring one segment to continue the spiral.

8. Check for spaces between rings. Sand if needed.

9. Glue the rings, clamp, and let dry.

10. Sand the inside of the bowl smooth.

11. Cut a ½" (13mm) plug from the scrap of purpleheart.

12. Drill a ½" (13mm) hole through the center of the base.

13. Glue the plug into place. Sand the base smooth.

14. Glue on the base, making sure the plug is centered. Clamp and let dry.

15. Sand the outside of the bowl.

16. Apply finish of choice.

**Multi-Colored Twenty Segment Bowl
Lamination Guide**
Copy at 125%

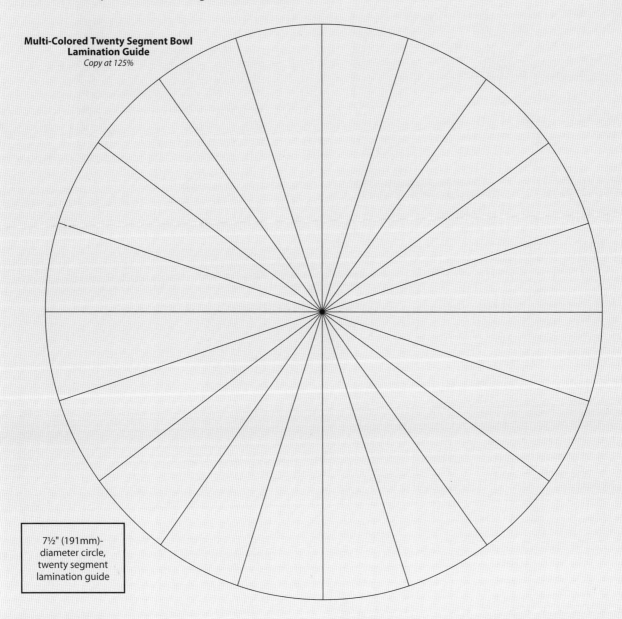

7½" (191mm)-diameter circle, twenty segment lamination guide

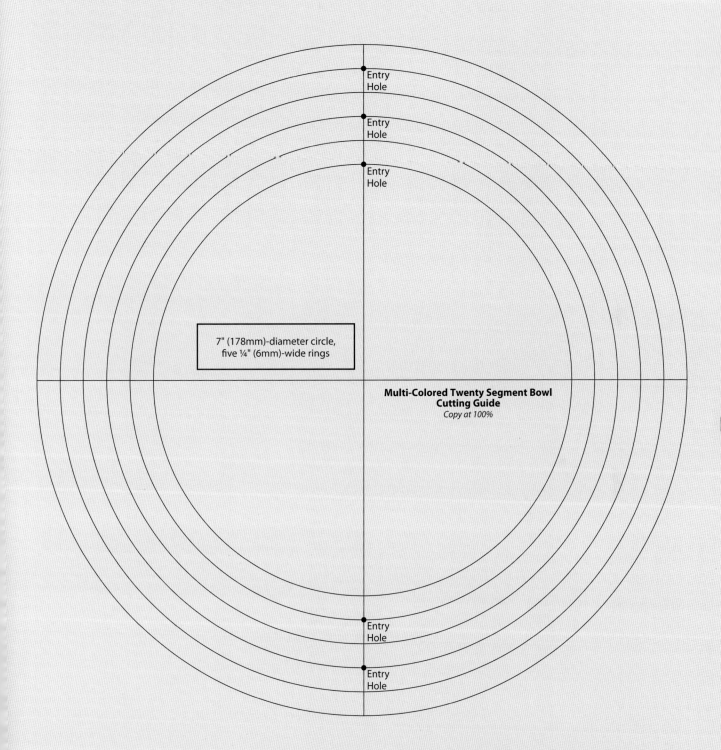

Entry
Hole

Entry
Hole

Entry
Hole

7" (178mm)-diameter circle,
five ¼" (6mm)-wide rings

**Multi-Colored Twenty Segment Bowl
Cutting Guide**
Copy at 100%

Entry
Hole

Entry
Hole

Seven-Lobe Ripple-Edged Bowl

Certain colors evoke specific images. This combination of oak, padauk, and walnut creates a fall palette, reminiscent of changing leaves. For a spring effect, I might have used yellowheart, purpleheart, and maple. The ripple edge adds additional interest with little extra effort.

I cut the bowl blank to a circle before gluing up the pieces to allow the use of the bowl press. I've found that thin woods tend to warp unless clamped securely, and that the best way to counteract that is with the even pressure the bowl press provides. If you are not using a bowl press, glue up the squares of wood, clamp conventionally, and proceed directly to making the bowl.

Materials and Tools

Wood
- (1) 7½" x 7½" x ⅛" (191mm x 191mm x 3mm) oak
- (1) 7½" x 7½" x ¼" (191mm x 191mm x 6mm) walnut
- (1) 7½" x 7½" x ⅛" (191mm x 191mm x 3mm) padauk

Materials
- Packing tape (optional)
- Glue
- Double-sided tape (if using a bowl press for the lamination)
- Repositionable adhesive
- Sanding discs for flexible pad sander, assorted grits 60 to 400
- Sandpaper for inflatable ball sander, assorted grits 60 to 320 (optional)
- Sandpaper for hand sanding, assorted grits 220 to 400
- 0000 steel wool or 320-grit sanding sponge
- Spray shellac or Danish oil

Tools
- Scroll saw blade, size #9
- Drill bit size #54 or ¹⁄₁₆" (2mm)
- Awl
- Ruler
- Compass
- Bowl press or clamps
- 2" (51mm) flexible pad sander
- Inflatable ball sander and pump (optional)

Lamination guide

1. Stack the wood, using double-sided tape at corners.

2. Using the compass, draw a circle 7½" (191mm) in diameter on the wood.

3. Cut along the circle through all three pieces of wood. Separate. Remove any tape stuck to the wood.

4. Glue up the wood circles (oak, walnut, then padauk), clamp, and let dry. Keep the grain of all pieces running in the same direction.

Making the bowl

1. Draw guidelines on the laminated blank, padauk side up.

2. Glue the pattern to the blank with repositionable adhesive, aligning guidelines.

3. Cut the outline at 28°, table left side down, cutting clockwise.

4. Drill a 28° entry hole. Complete the first ring, mark the top, and remove the pattern. Place the ring on the blank and transfer guidelines to the ring.

5. Use the first ring to mark the second ring.

6. Drill an entry hole and cut the second ring.

7. Use the second ring to mark the third ring.

8. Cut the third ring.

9. Glue up the rings, clamp, and let dry.

10. Sand the inside smooth.

11. Glue on the base, clamp, and let dry.

12. Sand the outside of the bowl and contour the upper rim.

13. Apply finish of choice.

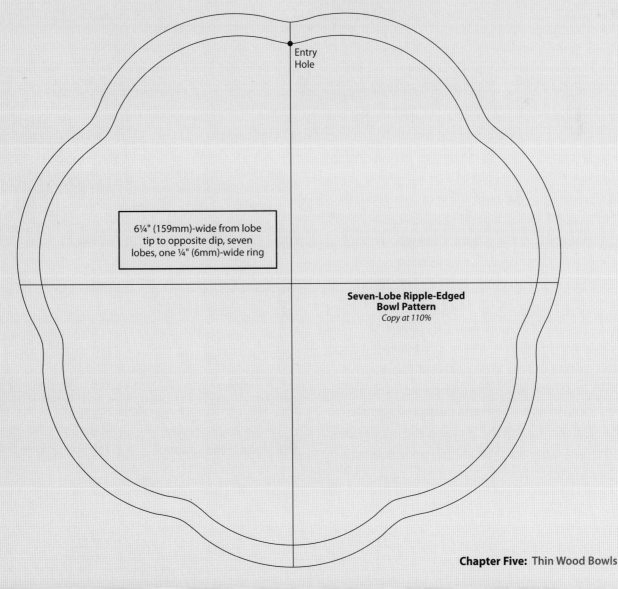

Entry
Hole

6¼" (159mm)-wide from lobe tip to opposite dip, seven lobes, one ¼" (6mm)-wide ring

**Seven-Lobe Ripple-Edged
Bowl Pattern**
Copy at 110%

91

I found an attractive piece of wood labeled "Santos Mahogany" in the "cutoff corner" of my favorite lumberyard. It had a pretty grain and color, but seemed quite dense. A little research revealed it came from Brazil, was used for flooring, and was 175% harder than red oak! However, since it was only ⅝" (16mm) thick, I decided to give it a try. I got off to a bad start when I broke a bit drilling the first entry hole. A piece of the bit embedded itself into the wood, so I drilled an additional hole and cut up to the bit. When it refused to budge, I hit the blank with a hammer—the ring broke loose and the bit fell out. The rest of the project proceeded without difficulty, but I was glad the design called for only two rings.

Materials and Tools

Wood
❖ (1) 9" x 7" x ⅝" (229mm x 178mm x 16mm) Santos mahogany

Materials
❖ Packing tape (optional)
❖ Glue
❖ Repositionable adhesive
❖ Sanding discs for flexible pad sander, assorted grits 60 to 400
❖ Sandpaper for inflatable ball sander, assorted grits 60 to 320 (optional)
❖ Sandpaper for hand sanding, assorted grits 220 to 400

❖ 0000 steel wool or 320-grit sanding sponge
❖ Spray shellac or Danish oil

Tools
❖ Scroll saw blade, size #9
❖ Drill bit size #54 or ¹⁄₁₆" (2mm)
❖ Awl
❖ Ruler
❖ Bowl press or clamps
❖ 2" (51mm) flexible pad sander
❖ Inflatable ball sander and pump (optional)

Making the bowl

1. Draw guidelines on the bowl blank.

2. Attach the pattern with repositionable adhesive, using the awl to center it on the guidelines.

3. Tilt the saw table 35°, left side down.

4. Cut along the outer ring, cutting clockwise.

5. Drill a 35° entry hole on the inner ring and cut clockwise to complete the first ring. Remove the pattern.

6. Place the first ring on the blank and transfer guidelines.

7. Use the first ring to draw the outline for the second ring.

8. Drill a 32° entry hole.

9. With the saw table tilted to 32°, left side down, cut out the second ring, cutting clockwise.

10. Stack the rings. Check for alignment and spaces.

11. Glue the rings, clamp, and let dry.

12. Sand the inside of the bowl smooth.

13. Glue on the base, clamp, and let dry.

14. Sand the outside of the bowl smooth. Flare the upper rim.

15. Apply finish of choice.

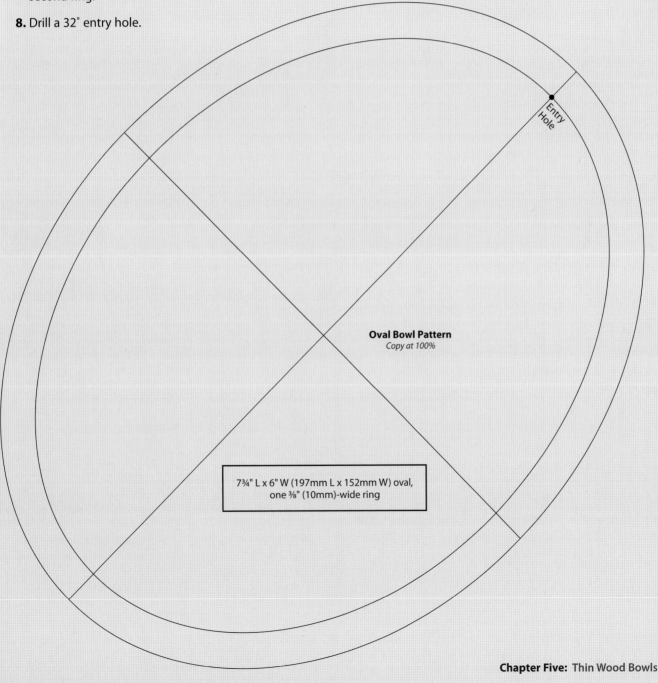

Entry Hole

Oval Bowl Pattern
Copy at 100%

7¾" L x 6" W (197mm L x 152mm W) oval,
one ⅜" (10mm)-wide ring

Center Lamination Bowl

This straight-sided rectangular bowl has thin walls that give it a delicate look. I chose a darker-colored wood for the center strip, but you can vary the color scheme to your preference. A Danish oil finish was used to highlight the functional appearance of this useful little bowl.

Materials and Tools

Wood
❖ (2) 8" x 3" x ⅝" (203mm x 76mm x 16mm) oak
❖ (1) 8" x 2" x ⅝" (203mm x 51mm x 16mm) Santos mahogany
❖ (2) 8" x ⅝" x ⅛" (203mm x 16mm x 3mm) maple

Materials
❖ Packing tape (optional)
❖ Glue
❖ Repositionable adhesive
❖ Sanding discs for flexible pad sander, assorted grits 60 to 400
❖ Sandpaper for inflatable ball sander, assorted grits 60 to 320 (optional)

❖ Sandpaper for hand sanding, assorted grits 220 to 400
❖ 0000 steel wool or 320-grit sanding sponge
❖ Spray shellac or Danish oil

Tools
❖ Scroll saw blade, size #9
❖ Drill bit size #54 or ¹⁄₁₆" (2mm)
❖ Awl
❖ Ruler
❖ Bowl press or clamps
❖ Clamps for lamination
❖ 2" (51mm) flexible pad sander
❖ Inflatable ball sander and pump (optional)

Lamination guide

1. Glue up the wood strips in the following order: oak, maple, mahogany, maple, oak. It's a good idea to clamp an additional piece of wood across the lamination to keep the blank flat. Clamp and let dry.

Making the bowl

1. Draw guidelines on the bowl blank.

2. Attach the pattern with repositionable adhesive, using an awl to center it on the guidelines.

3. Tilt the saw table to 23°, left side down.

4. Cut along the outer ring, cutting clockwise.

5. Drill a 23° entry hole and cut along the inner ring to complete the first ring. Remove the pattern.

6. Place the first ring on the blank and mark the top and guidelines on the ring.

7. Trace the outline for the second ring.

8. Drill an entry hole and cut the second ring.

9. Place the second ring on the blank and mark the top and guidelines on the ring.

10. Trace the outline for the third ring.

11. Drill an entry hole and cut the third ring.

12. Stack the rings and check for alignment and spaces.

13. Glue the rings, clamp, and let dry.

14. Sand the inside of the bowl smooth.

15. Glue on the base, clamp, and let dry.

16. Sand the outside of the bowl smooth.

17. Apply finish of choice.

95

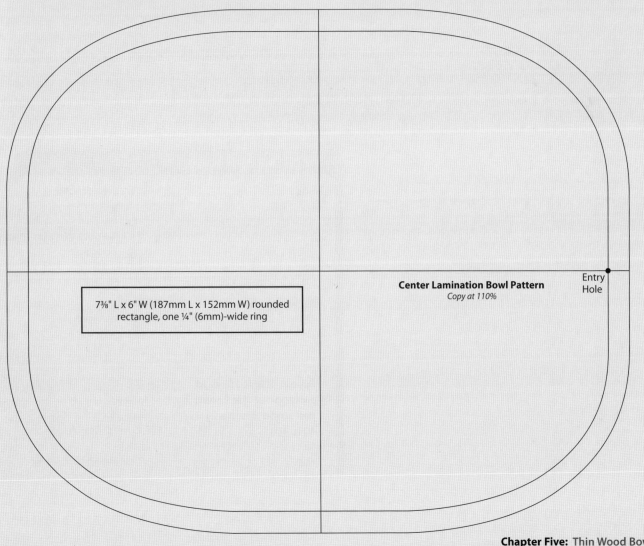

7⅜" L x 6" W (187mm L x 152mm W) rounded rectangle, one ¼" (6mm)-wide ring

Center Lamination Bowl Pattern
Copy at 110%

Entry Hole

I wanted to use a floral color for this petal-shaped bowl, and thought that purpleheart, set off by oak, would be a good choice. Layering the purpleheart on top produced a purple top band and intensely colored base interior, which was just the effect I wanted.

Materials and Tools

Wood
- (1) 8" x 8" x ½" (203mm x 203mm x 13mm) oak
- (1) 8" x 8" x ⅛" (203mm x 203mm x 3mm) purpleheart

Materials
- Packing tape (optional)
- Glue
- Double-sided tape (if using bowl press for lamination)
- Repositionable adhesive
- Sanding discs for flexible pad sander, assorted grits 60 to 400
- Sandpaper for inflatable ball sander, assorted grits 60 to 320 (optional)
- Sandpaper for hand sanding, assorted grits 220 to 400
- 0000 steel wool or 320-grit sanding sponge
- Spray shellac or Danish oil

Tools
- Scroll saw blade, size #9
- Drill bit size #54 or ¹⁄₁₆" (2mm)
- Awl
- Ruler
- Compass
- Bowl press or clamps
- 2" (51mm) flexible pad sander
- Inflatable ball sander and pump (optional)

Lamination guide

1. If using a bowl press to clamp the lamination, attach the two squares of wood with double-sided tape.

2. Use the compass to draw a 7½" (191mm) circle on the wood. Cut out the circles and separate them.

3. Glue the two circles together. Be sure to keep the grain of both pieces running in the same direction. Clamp and let dry overnight.

4. If not using a bowl press, glue and clamp the squares of wood conventionally and proceed directly to making the bowl.

Making the bowl

1. With the purpleheart side up, draw guidelines on the bowl blank.

2. Glue the pattern to the laminated blank with repositionable adhesive, using the awl to center the pattern on the guidelines.

3. Cut along the outer line with the saw table at a 23° angle, left side down, cutting clockwise.

4. Drill an entry hole at 23°. Cut along the inner line to complete the first ring. Remove the pattern.

5. Place the first ring on the blank.

6. Mark the top, transfer the guidelines, and mark the outline of the second ring.

7. Cut and mark the second and third rings in the same manner.

8. Glue up the rings, clamp, and let dry.

9. Sand the inside smooth.

10. Glue on the base, clamp, and let dry.

11. Sand the outside of the bowl smooth and contour the rim.

12. Apply finish of choice.

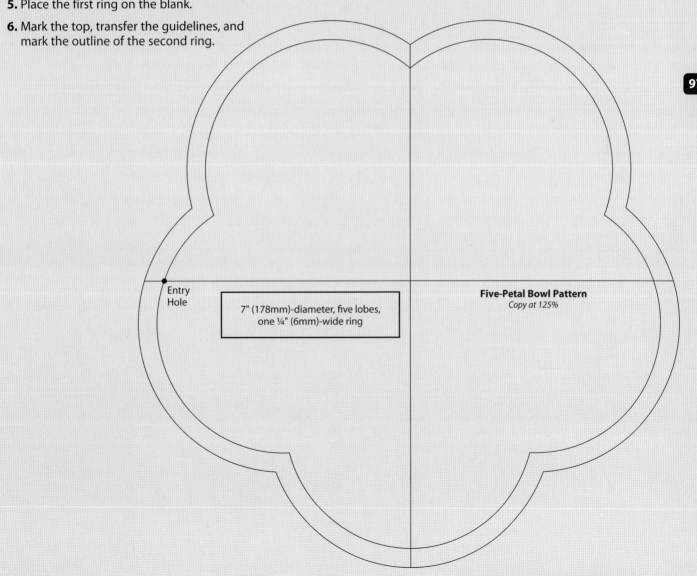

Entry
Hole

7" (178mm)-diameter, five lobes,
one ¼" (6mm)-wide ring

Five-Petal Bowl Pattern
Copy at 125%

6

Thinking Outside the Bowl

While a great deal of variety can be achieved using a single set of rings, a whole world opens up when you add additional sets. Two straight bowls stacked top to top become a modern vase, a curved bowl stacked on a straight one becomes a ginger jar, and a straight ring glued to an angled one becomes a base for a candy dish. Ring sets can be of the same or contrasting woods. Plain or laminated blanks can be used. Rings of different thicknesses can be inserted. This chapter explores some of the possibilities that emerge when you think "outside the bowl."

Many types of projects other than bowls can be created with the stacked ring method.

This easy-to-make vase is a good introduction to projects constructed from multiple sets of rings. It consists of two sets of straight-sided rings glued together and topped with a set of rings that have been shaped with both spindle and inflatable ball sanders. I suspected cherry and mahogany would provide an attractive contrast; the flecks of sapwood that appeared in the cherry were an unexpected bonus.

Materials and Tools

Wood

Vase body:
- ❖ (1) 8" x 8" x ¾" (203mm x 203mm x 19mm) cherry
- ❖ (1) 8" x 8" x ¾" (203mm x 203mm x 19mm) mahogany

Base:
- ❖ (1) 5" x 2½" x ¼" (127mm x 64mm x 6mm) mahogany
- ❖ (1) 5" x 2½" x ¼" (127mm x 64mm x 6mm) cherry

Neck:
- ❖ (1) 4" x 2" x ¾" (102mm x 51mm x 19mm) mahogany
- ❖ (1) 4" x 2" x ¾" (102mm x 51mm x 19mm) cherry

Materials

- ❖ Packing tape (optional)
- ❖ Glue
- ❖ Repositionable adhesive
- ❖ Sanding discs for flexible pad sander, assorted grits 60 to 400
- ❖ Sandpaper for inflatable ball sander, assorted grits 60 to 320
- ❖ Sandpaper for hand sanding, assorted grits 220 to 400
- ❖ 0000 steel wool or 320-grit sanding sponge
- ❖ Spray shellac or Danish oil

Tools

- ❖ Scroll saw blade, size #9
- ❖ Drill bit size #54 or ¹⁄₁₆" (2mm)
- ❖ Awl
- ❖ Ruler
- ❖ Compass
- ❖ Clamps for lamination
- ❖ Bowl press or clamps
- ❖ 2" (51mm) flexible pad sander
- ❖ Inflatable ball sander and pump

Lamination guide

1. Cut the 8" (203mm) pieces of mahogany and cherry in half, cutting along the grain. Number the pieces as shown (right). These pieces will form the vase body lamination.

2. Create two multi-color 8" x 8" (203mm x 203mm) laminated blanks for the vase body by gluing the edges of pieces 1 and 2 together, and the edges of pieces 3 and 4 together. Clamp them and let dry.

3. Mark the top of each blank and sand flat if needed.

4. Glue together the 5" x 2½" x ¼" (127mm x 64mm x 6mm) pieces of cherry and mahogany to make a 5" x 5" x ¼" (127mm x 127mm x 6mm) lamination for the vase base. Rub the edges together to obtain a good bond. Let dry.

5. Glue together the 4" x 2" x ¾" (102mm x 51mm x 19mm) pieces of cherry and mahogany to make a 4" x 4" x ¾" (102mm x 102mm x 19mm) lamination for the vase neck. Clamp and let dry.

Step 1

Prepare the wood for the vase body lamination.

Keeping laminations flat

To keep larger laminations flat as they dry, clamp a piece of wood across the lamination. Be sure to use waxed paper under the cross piece to prevent it from sticking to the lamination.

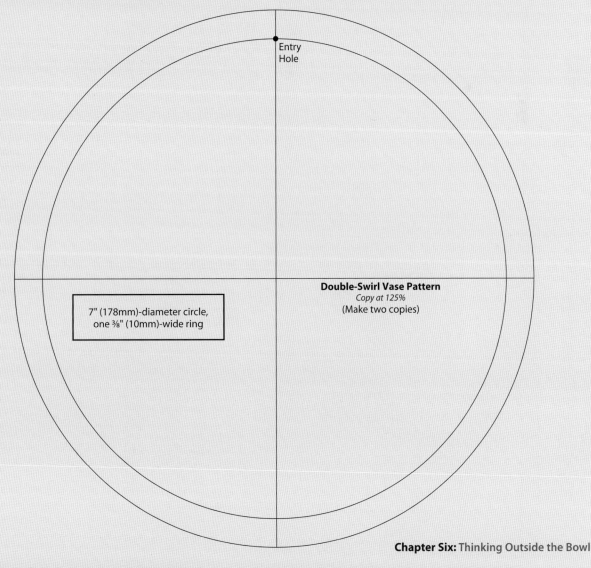

Entry
Hole

Double-Swirl Vase Pattern
Copy at 125%
(Make two copies)

7" (178mm)-diameter circle,
one ⅜" (10mm)-wide ring

Making the vase

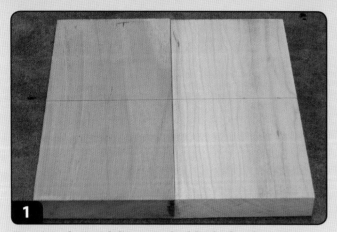

1

Drawing the guidelines on the blanks for the vase body. Mark the midpoints of the sides of each 8" x 8" (203mm x 203mm) laminated blank and draw lines to form intersecting guidelines.

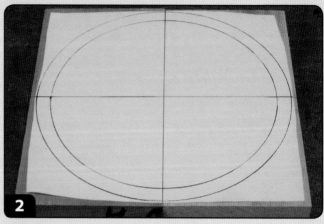

2

Gluing on the vase body pattern. Glue on a vase body pattern with repositionable adhesive to each of the two blanks, using an awl to center the pattern. Align the guidelines on the pattern and the wood. Mark the top.

3

Cutting the outer profile of the vase body. Tilt the saw table 28°, left side down. Cut the profile of both blanks clockwise along the outer line.

4

Marking the top. Mark the tops of both body pieces. As you continue, be sure to mark each ring set clearly— mark all of one set with a number 1, and the other with a number 2.

5

Drilling the entry holes in the first ring. Using a tilting drill press or 28° angle guide, drill entry holes on the inner ring for both blanks at a 28° angle.

Note: Because the bowls that form the body of the vase are identical to the Basic Bowl in Chapter 2, page 22, you can use that pattern (page 27) to cut the four rings instead of using the ring method, if you prefer.

6 **Completing the first vase body ring.** Insert the saw blade into the entry hole and cut clockwise along the line to complete the ring. Mark the top of the ring. Repeat for the second vase body blank. Remove the patterns.

7 **Drawing the second vase body rings.** Place the first ring on the blank and transfer the guidelines from the blank to the sides of the ring and mark the top. Holding the ring in place, trace the inside of the ring on the blank to use as a cutting line for the second ring. Repeat for the second vase body blank.

8 **Drilling the second entry hole.** Mark a point on the second ring opposite the first entry hole. Drill an entry hole at a 28° angle. Repeat for the second vase body blank.

9 **Cutting the remaining rings.** Cut out and mark the second ring for both vase body blanks. Cut out and mark the third and fourth rings for both blanks in the same manner. Be sure to keep each ring set clearly marked.

10 **Preparing the rings for gluing.** Stack each set of rings in a spiral pattern and check for spaces between the rings. Sand as needed. Remove any pencil marks from the lower inner edges and top surfaces of the rings.

11 **Gluing the rings.** For each set, glue the four rings together, keeping the spiral pattern even. Clamp and let dry. You will have one piece left over from each set of rings. Be sure to mark which piece belongs to each set. These two pieces will be used to form the top assembly in Steps 17–24.

Making the vase (continued)

12

Sanding the inside of the rings. Sand the inside of each set of rings just until ridges are smoothed out. They do not need to be finely sanded. Use either a flexible pad or inflatable ball sander, or a spindle sander with the table tilted to 28°. Be sure to leave the rings at least ¼" (6mm)-wide at the top and bottom edges to have enough wood for gluing and shaping.

13

Sanding the outside of the rings. Sand the outside of each set of rings until any ridges are smoothed out. You will complete the sanding later. You can use either a vertical sander with the table set to 28° or a flexible pad sander. Be sure to leave the rings at least ¼" (6mm)-wide at the top and bottom edges to have enough wood for gluing and shaping.

14

Cutting the base. Decide which set of rings to use for the lower half of the vase body. Center that set of rings on the glued-up base lamination. Trace the outline of the bottom ring onto the base piece. Tilt the scroll saw table to 28°, left side down, and cut the base clockwise on that line. Cut generously to the outside of the line.

15

Gluing on the base. Glue the base to the bottom of the ring set whose outline you traced. Be sure to continue the spiral pattern. Clamp and let dry. Sand the base flush with the sides.

16

Completing the body of the vase. Invert the set of rings without the base (now called the top set) on the set with the base (now called the bottom set). Be sure to continue the spiral pattern. Glue together and weight down. Let dry.

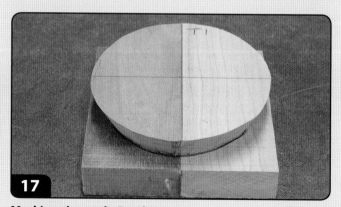

17

Marking the neck. For this step, use the leftover piece from Step 11 that belongs to the top set of rings. (The other piece will be used in Step 21.) Place this piece, larger side up, on the laminated piece for the neck, aligning the laminations. Trace the outline.

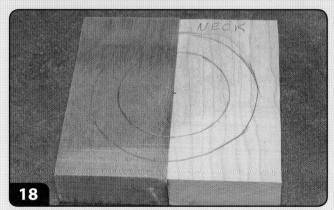

18

Cutting the neck. Mark the center of the circle you drew in Step 17. Using a compass, place the point on this center mark and draw a circle that is 1" (25mm) smaller than this circle. This will give you a ring that is about ½" (13mm) wide. With the saw table level, cut along the outer line. Drill a straight entry hole just inside the inner line and cut out the center. Discard the center.

19

Marking the lower part of the top assembly. Place the angled piece used in Step 17 so the larger face is down. Center the neckpiece on top of the angled piece and trace the inner circle. This is the cutting line.

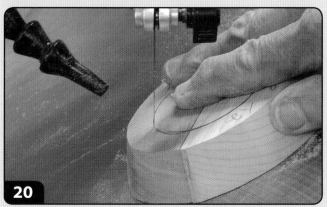

20

Cutting the lower part of the top assembly. Drill an entry hole about ¼" (6mm) inside the cutting line at 28°, angled toward the *outside* of the piece. Tilt the scroll saw table 28°, left side down. Insert the saw blade and cut *counterclockwise* along the line. This piece is the lower part of the top assembly.

21

Cutting the upper part of the top assembly. Repeat Steps 19 and 20 with the remaining piece from Step 11. This piece will be the upper part of the top assembly.

22

Gluing the top assembly. Glue together the lower part of the top assembly, the neckpiece, and the upper part of the top assembly, continuing the spiral. Clamp and let dry.

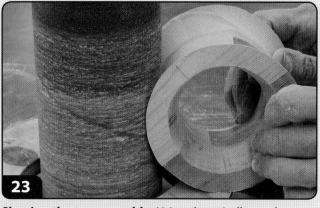

23

Shaping the top assembly. Using the spindle sander, smooth the center hole of the neckpiece, and then turn the top assembly on its side to sand in a curved shape.

Making the vase *(continued)*

24

Contouring the top assembly. Using the inflatable ball sander, smooth the inside join with the neckpiece and contour and thin the upper rim.

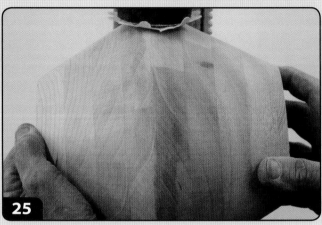

25

Rough-shaping the vase body. Using the flexible pad sander, smooth the join between the vase body ring sets. Feel inside as you sand to be sure you don't remove too much wood.

26

Gluing the top assembly to the top set of rings. Place the top assembly on the top set of rings, continuing the spiral. Glue together. Place weight on top and let dry.

27

Finishing the sanding and shaping. Using the flexible pad sander, finish shaping and sanding the outside of vase, using progressively finer grits.

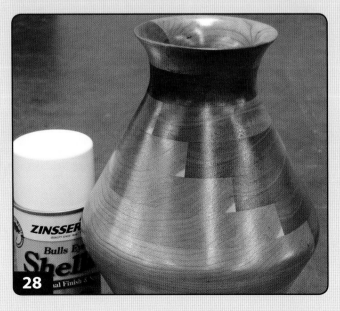

28

Finishing the vase. Give the sanded vase several coats of shellac, smoothing between each coat with a 320-grit flexible sanding sponge or 0000 steel wool.

Wooden Bowls from the Scroll Saw

Ginger Jar

A ceramic ginger jar lamp on a brass base served as the model for this project. The jar itself was not difficult to replicate—it's simply a small curved bowl inverted on a straight one with a straight ring between—but the cutout sides of the base posed a challenge. The solution was simple once I realized that by using a single square of wood, cut diagonally into four pieces and trimmed, I could make compound cuts on the sides to create the pattern I wanted.

When making the jar, it's important to keep the grain of the different ring sets running in the same direction. This helps create the illusion that the jar is cut from a single piece of wood. I chose teak for the base, but another dark wood, like walnut, could be used.

Materials and Tools

Wood

Jar:
- (3) 7" x 7" x ¾" (178mm x 178mm x 19mm) maple

Lid:
- (1) 4" x 4" x ¼" (102mm x 102mm x 6mm) maple

Base:
- (1) 5½" x 5½" x ¾" (140mm x 140mm x 19mm) teak

Base ring:
- (1) 4½" x 4½" x ¼" (114mm x 114mm x 6mm) teak

Materials
- Packing tape (optional)
- Glue
- Repositionable adhesive
- Sanding discs for flexible pad sander, assorted grits 60 to 400
- Sandpaper for inflatable ball sander, assorted grits 60 to 320 (optional)
- Sandpaper for hand sanding, assorted grits 220 to 400
- 0000 steel wool or 320-grit sanding sponge
- Spray shellac or Danish oil
- Rubber band for clamping base
- Blue tape for masking base

Tools
- Scroll saw blade, size #9
- Drill bit size #54 or 1/16" (2mm)
- Awl
- Ruler
- Bowl press or clamps
- 2" (51mm) flexible pad sander
- Inflatable ball sander and pump (optional)

Making ring set 1

1. For the first set of rings, which forms the bottom part of the jar, draw guidelines on one of the 7" (178mm) pieces of maple and glue on the pattern for ring set 1 (page 109) with repositionable adhesive.

2. With the scroll saw table tilted 20°, left side down, cut clockwise along the outer circle. Drill a 20° entry hole on the inner circle and make the cut to complete the first ring.

3. Place the first ring on the blank. Transfer the guidelines, mark the top, and trace the outline of the second ring. Drill a 20° entry hole and cut out the second ring. Use the second ring to mark the third ring.

4. Cut out the third ring. You now have three rings—each ¼" (6mm) wide—and a base.

5. Glue up the rings, clamp, and let dry.

6. Sand the inside lightly with a flexible pad or inflatable ball sander to smooth any ridges. Keep the sides as thick as possible to allow for shaping of the outside of the jar.

7. Glue on the base, clamp, and let dry.

Making the center ring

1. For the center ring, which will go between the top and the bottom ring sets of the jar, glue the pattern for the center ring (page 109) to a second piece of 7" (178mm) maple with repositionable adhesive.

2. Cut along the outer circle with the saw table level.

3. Drill a straight entry hole just inside the inner ring and cut out the ring. You will have a straight-sided single ring, ½" (13mm) wide. Reserve the center piece that is left for making the top lip and lid.

Making ring set 2

1. For the second set of rings, which will become the top of the jar, draw guidelines on the third 7" (178mm) piece of maple.

2. Glue on the pattern for ring set 2 (page 109) with repositionable adhesive.

3. Cut along the outer circle with the saw table set at 34°, left side down, cutting clockwise.

4. Drill a 34° entry hole on the inner circle and complete the ring. You will have one ½" (13mm)-wide ring and a base.

5. Glue the ring to the base, clamp, and let dry.

6. Sand the inside lightly. Invert so that the bottom side is up. This will be the top of the jar.

Making the lip and lid

1. Glue lid pattern (page 111) with repositionable adhesive to the piece saved from the center ring.

2. Drill a straight entry hole just inside the innermost ring and cut out the center with the saw table level. This center piece will not be used for this project.

3. Drill a straight entry hole on the next circle and cut along the line to complete the lip of the jar.

4. Sand the lip smooth. This is the part of the jar that the lid will fit over.

5. Sand the sides of the circle left in the remaining piece. Glue this piece to the ¼" (6mm)-thick piece of maple. Keep the grain of both pieces running in the same direction. Clamp and let dry.

6. Cut along the outer ring. This piece is the lid. When inverted, it will fit nicely over the lip.

7. Sand to soften the top and bottom edges of the lid, and the top edge of the lip.

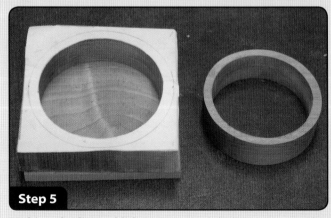

Step 5

Making the lip and lid, Step 5. The lid, shown next to the lip, is ready for cutting.

Assembling the jar

1. Center the lip on the top of the jar (inverted ring set 2), aligning the grain, and trace the inside. This should be about a 2" (51mm) circle.

2. Drill a straight entry hole just inside the circle. With the saw table level, cut out the circle.

3. Glue the lip in place, keeping the grains aligned. Weight down and let dry.

4. Sand the inside of the lip flush with the inside of the jar.

5. Glue the center ring to ring set 2 (top of the jar), keeping grains aligned. Clamp and let dry.

6. Glue this assembly to ring set 1 (bottom of jar), keeping grains aligned. Weight down and let dry.

7. Place the lid over the lip and trace the outline. Keep the area inside the outline flat so the lid will sit flush with the jar. Sand the outside of the jar with the flexible pad sander, checking your work carefully for shape and symmetry, and using progressively finer grits.

8. Apply finish of choice. Keep underside unfinished for gluing to base.

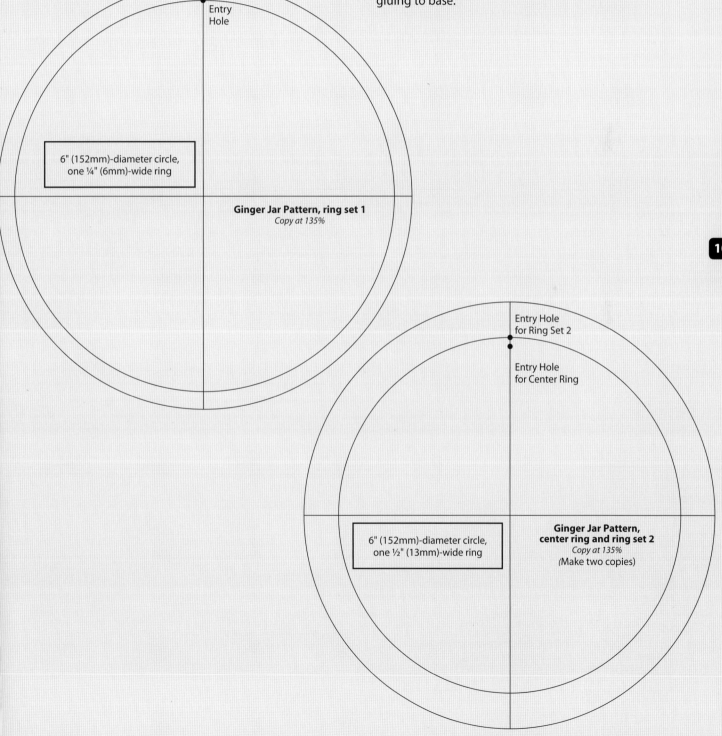

Entry Hole

6" (152mm)-diameter circle, one ¼" (6mm)-wide ring

Ginger Jar Pattern, ring set 1
Copy at 135%

Entry Hole for Ring Set 2

Entry Hole for Center Ring

6" (152mm)-diameter circle, one ½" (13mm)-wide ring

Ginger Jar Pattern, center ring and ring set 2
Copy at 135%
(Make two copies)

Making the base

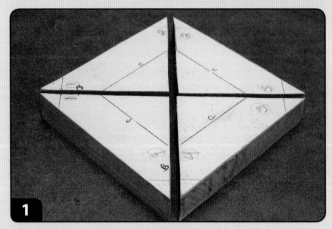

1

Cutting the outline and diagonals. You will need two copies of the top pattern (page 112) and four of the side pattern (page 112). Glue the base top pattern to the 5½" (140mm) piece of teak with repositionable adhesive and cut along the outline (A). Cut along the diagonals (B) to form four pieces. Mark the pieces as shown so you can reassemble them properly later.

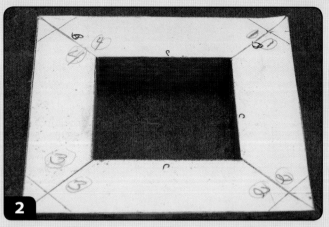

2

Cutting the inner lines. Cut along the inner lines (C).

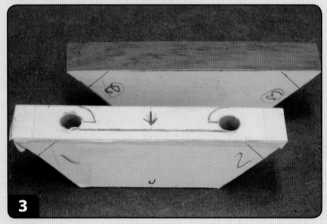

3

Laying out the sides. Glue a copy of the base side pattern (page 112, top) or the alternate base side pattern (page 112, bottom) with repositionable adhesive to the outside face of each piece. Drill two ⅜" (10mm) holes where indicated.

4

Cutting the sides. Cut along the pattern lines. Use supports if desired.

5

Gluing the base. Remove the patterns. Glue the four pieces together. Clamp with a rubber band and let dry.

6

Shaping the base. Use the base top pattern as a guide for cutting off the four corners. Round the corners and soften the top edges.

7

Cutting the beveled circle. Place the ginger jar on the 4½" (114mm) piece of teak and trace the lower profile. Tilt the saw table 20°, left side down, and cut along the line *counterclockwise*. This will give you an outward flaring circle with a top diameter that matches the bottom of the jar. Glue the circle to the top of the base. Weight down and let dry. Sand smooth.

8

Finishing the base. Cover the face of the circle with blue tape, leaving a small outer edge uncovered. Apply finish of choice to base. Remove the tape. Glue the ginger jar to the base, weight down, and let dry.

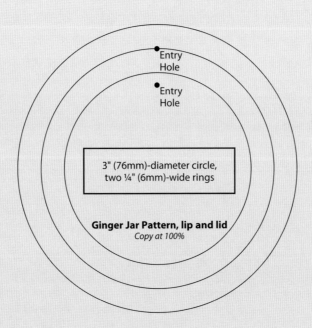

Entry
Hole

Entry
Hole

3" (76mm)-diameter circle,
two ¼" (6mm)-wide rings

Ginger Jar Pattern, lip and lid
Copy at 100%

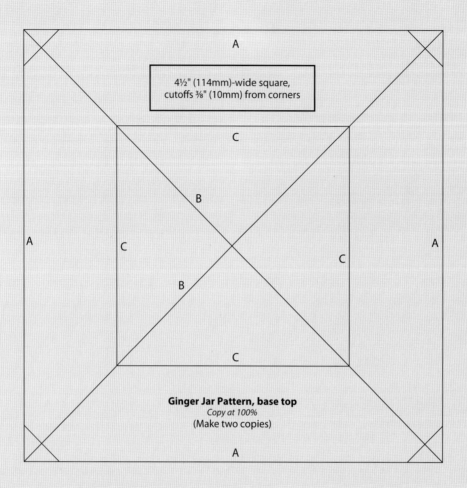

4½" (114mm)-wide square,
cutoffs ⅜" (10mm) from corners

Ginger Jar Pattern, base top
Copy at 100%
(Make two copies)

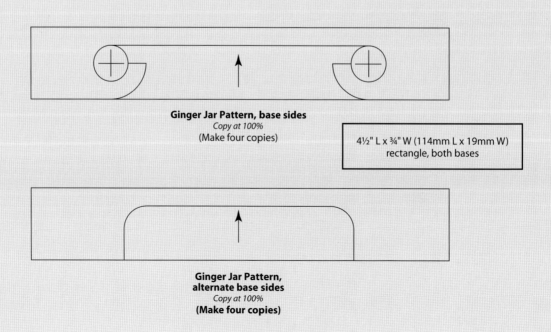

Ginger Jar Pattern, base sides
Copy at 100%
(Make four copies)

4½" L x ¾" W (114mm L x 19mm W)
rectangle, both bases

**Ginger Jar Pattern,
alternate base sides**
Copy at 100%
(Make four copies)

If you enjoy freehand sanding, this is the piece for you! The rounded shape is achieved through a combination of angled cutting and sanding. Beveling the angled rings that surround the center ring allows that ring to protrude slightly. This makes it easier to keep the symmetry as you shape the center of the piece. Since the inward curving shape limits access for sanding the interior, the rings are not glued up all at once. An inflatable ball sander is used for smoothing the insides.

I decided to use a laminated center ring, but any contrasting piece of ¾" to 1" (19mm to 25mm)-thick wood can be substituted. Instead of a lid, you can finish the top opening with a rim that matches the color of the center ring.

For maximum attractiveness, be sure to keep the grain of all rings running in the same direction.

Materials and Tools

Wood

Jar:
- ❖ (2) 7" x 7" x ¾" (178mm x 178mm x 19mm) walnut

Lamination:
- ❖ (1) 7" x 7" x ¾" (178mm x 178mm x 19mm) maple
- ❖ (2) 7" x 7" x ⅛" (178mm x 178mm x 3mm) padauk

Lid rim and insert:
- ❖ (1) 4" x 4" x ¼" (102mm x 102mm x 6mm) walnut

Lid:
- ❖ (1) 4" x 4" x ¾" (102mm x 102mm x 19mm) maple

Base:
- ❖ (1) 5" x 5" x ¾" (127mm x 127mm x 19mm) maple

Materials

- ❖ Packing tape (optional)
- ❖ Glue
- ❖ Repositionable adhesive
- ❖ Sanding discs for flexible pad sander, assorted grits 60 to 400
- ❖ Sandpaper for inflatable ball sander, assorted grits 60 to 320
- ❖ Sandpaper for hand sanding, assorted grits 220 to 400
- ❖ 0000 steel wool or 320-grit sanding sponge
- ❖ Spray shellac or Danish oil
- ❖ Rubber band for clamping base
- ❖ Blue tape for masking base

Tools

- ❖ Scroll saw blade, size #9
- ❖ Drill bit size #54 or ¹⁄₁₆" (2mm)
- ❖ Awl
- ❖ Ruler
- ❖ Compass
- ❖ Bowl press or clamps
- ❖ 2" (51mm) flexible pad sander
- ❖ Inflatable ball sander and pump

Making the jar

1. Glue the pieces of padauk to each side of the 7" (178mm) piece of maple, keeping the grains running in the same direction. Clamp and let dry.

2. Glue the pattern (page 117) to the lamination with repositionable adhesive and cut along the outer circle with the table level.

3. Drill a straight entry hole, slightly inside the inner circle, and cut along the inner line with the table level. This forms the center ring. The center piece is not used for this project, but should be saved for future use.

4. Draw guidelines on the two 7" (178mm) pieces of walnut.

5. Glue the pattern (page 117) to each piece with repositionable adhesive, using the awl to center the pattern.

6. For each piece, cut along the outline at a 34° angle, table tilted left side down, cutting clockwise.

7. Drill 34° entry holes and complete the cutting of the rings. Mark the tops and transfer guidelines. Label each set so you don't mix up the rings.

8. Place each of these rings wide side up and draw a circle on each ring about ⅛" (3mm) from the outer edge. Tilt the saw table to 15°, left side down, and cut clockwise along this circle.

9. Pair up each beveled ring with its matching solid piece. Mark one set T, for the top half. Mark the other set B, for the bottom half.

10. Glue the laminated ring to the wider face of the ring from set T. Keep grains running in the same direction. Clamp and let dry. Sand the inside smooth.

11. Glue the ring from set B to the other side of the laminated ring. Keep grains running in the same direction. Clamp and let dry. Sand the inside smooth.

12. Rough shape the outside to round the laminated ring.

13. Glue on the solid piece from ring set B. Clamp and let dry. Do not glue on the solid piece from ring set T yet.

14. Place the solid piece from ring set T smaller side up. Draw a 2½" (64mm) circle in the center.

15. Drill an entry hole and cut out the center. You've just created the opening of the jar.

16. Sand the underside of the opening at an angle with the inflatable ball sander to bevel it slightly. This will make the inside more attractive.

17. Glue this piece to the rest of the jar, keeping the grains oriented. Clamp and let dry.

18. Finish shaping and sanding the outside of the jar. Leave about ⅜" (10mm) around the top opening flat to accommodate the rim.

Step 8

Cut around the first rings about ⅛" (3mm) in from the edge.

Step 10

Glue the center ring to ring T and sand.

Step 16

Sand the underside of the opening.

114

Making the rim and insert

1. To make the rim of the jar and the insert (the part of the lid that fits inside the rim), glue one copy of the lid and rim pattern (below) to the ¼" (6mm) piece of walnut with repositionable adhesive.

2. Drill a straight entry hole on the inner circle and cut out the center, with the saw table level. This will become the lid insert.

3. Cut along the outer line to complete the rim.

4. Sand both pieces smooth.

5. Center the rim on the top opening of the jar, glue into place, weight down, and let dry.

6. Sand the opening until the inside of the rim is flush with the inside of the jar.

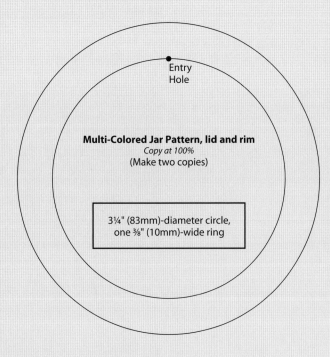

Entry
Hole

Multi-Colored Jar Pattern, lid and rim
Copy at 100%
(Make two copies)

3¼" (83mm)-diameter circle,
one ⅜" (10mm)-wide ring

Making the lid

1. To make the lid, glue another copy of the lid and rim pattern (page 115) to the 4" (102mm) piece of maple with repositionable adhesive and cut along the outer circle with the saw table level.

2. To bevel the lid, cut along the inner circle at a 45° angle, with the saw table left side down, cutting *counterclockwise*. This will create a bevel that will help you shape the lid. If your saw table will not tilt to a full 45° because of the thickness of the wood, tilt it as far as you can.

3. Sand the top and sides of the lid to a nicely rounded shape.

4. Center the lid insert on the underside of the lid and glue it into place. Invert the jar over the insert to check position, and adjust if needed.

5. Finish the bowl as desired. Keep the underside unfinished if gluing it to the base.

Step 2

Bevel the edge of the lid at a 45° angle.

Step 4

Glue the insert in the center of the lid underside.

Making the base

1. You will need two copies of the base top pattern (page 117) and four copies of the base side pattern (page 117).

2. Glue the top pattern to the 5" (127mm) piece of maple with repositionable adhesive.

3. Cut along the outline (A).

4. Cut along the diagonals (B).

5. Cut along the inner lines (C).

6. Mark the adjacent pieces so you can assemble them later.

7. Glue the side pattern to each piece with repositionable adhesive and cut out the center piece.

8. Glue the pieces together. Use a rubber band to clamp, and let dry.

9. Glue on the top pattern with repositionable adhesive and cut out the circle with the saw table level.

10. Sand the base smooth. Soften the edges of the top and of the cutouts.

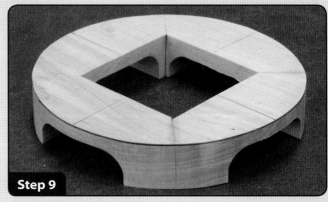

Step 9

Cut the base into a circle.

11. Mask the center of the base with blue painter's tape and apply finish of choice. Remove the tape.

12. Glue the jar to the base, weight down, and let dry.

116

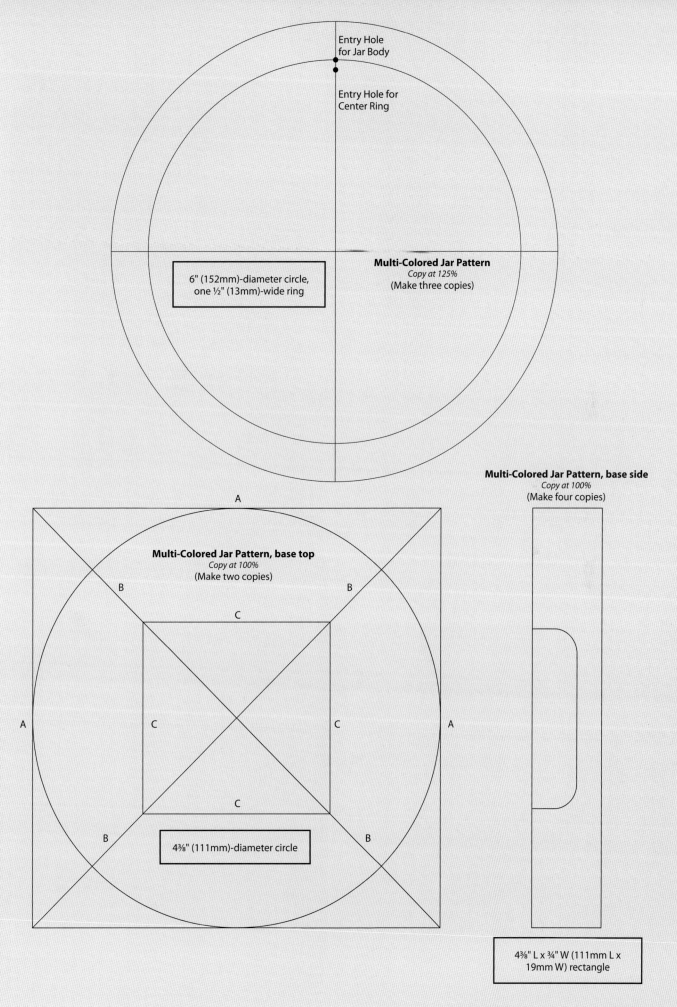

Entry Hole
for Jar Body

Entry Hole for
Center Ring

Multi-Colored Jar Pattern
Copy at 125%
(Make three copies)

6" (152mm)-diameter circle,
one ½" (13mm)-wide ring

A

Multi-Colored Jar Pattern, base top
Copy at 100%
(Make two copies)

B   B

C

C   C

A   A

C

B   B

4⅜" (111mm)-diameter circle

Multi-Colored Jar Pattern, base side
Copy at 100%
(Make four copies)

4⅜" L x ¾" W (111mm L x
19mm W) rectangle

Chapter Six: Thinking Outside the Bowl

Footed Candy Dish

At a juried crafts show I attended, the large number of lathe-turned bowls that combined bloodwood and cherry to good effect impressed me. This project uses that combination to create an easy-to-make footed candy dish with a scalloped edge. Both cherry and bloodwood are dense and tend to burn, but if you use tape and change blades frequently, you should not have a problem. Also, the rings are generous in width and any burn marks can easily be sanded away.

The initial appearance of the scallops is somewhat alarming: while those on the outside take shape immediately, those on the inside won't look right until you contour the inside of the rim.

Because of the steep angle of the first ring, the outer edge of the second ring must be recut to avoid the need for excessive sanding.

Materials and Tools

Wood
Dish:
- (1) 7" x 7" x ¾" (178mm x 178mm x 19mm) cherry
- (4) 3" x ½" x ¾" (76mm x 13mm x 19mm) bloodwood
- (4) 5" x ½" x ¾" (127mm x 13mm x 19mm) bloodwood

Pedestal base:
- (1) 4" x 4" x ¾" (102mm x 102mm x 19mm) cherry
- (1) 3" x 3" x ¾" (76mm x 76mm x 19mm) cherry

Materials
- Packing tape
- Glue
- Repositionable adhesive
- Sanding discs for flexible pad sander, assorted grits 60 to 400
- Sandpaper for inflatable ball sander, assorted grits 60 to 320 (optional)
- Sandpaper for hand sanding, assorted grits 220 to 400
- 0000 steel wool or 320-grit sanding sponge
- Spray shellac or Danish oil

Tools
- Scroll saw blade, size #9
- Drill bit size #54 or ¹⁄₁₆" (2mm)
- Awl
- Ruler
- Compass
- Bowl press or clamps
- Clamps for lamination
- 2" (51mm) flexible pad sander
- Inflatable ball sander and pump (optional)

Wooden Bowls from the Scroll Saw

Lamination guide

1. Glue the lamination pattern and guide (below) to the 7" (178mm) piece of cherry with repositionable adhesive and cut out the perimeter.

2. Mark the center of the blank with a small awl mark.

3. Sand the edges smooth.

4. Refer to the lamination pattern and guide (below) to apply the bloodwood border. Glue two 3" pieces of bloodwood to opposite sides of the octagon (A). Clamp and let dry.

5. Glue two 3" (76mm) pieces of bloodwood to the set of opposite sides (B). Clamp and let dry.

6. Trim the bloodwood so the edges are flush with the unglued sides. You now have two sets of opposite sides that do not yet have bloodwood glued to them—C and D.

7. Glue two 5" (127mm) pieces of bloodwood to the set of opposite sides (C). Clamp and let dry.

8. Glue the last two 5" (127mm) pieces to the remaining set of sides (D). Clamp and let dry.

9. Trim the bloodwood so the edges are flush.

10. Sand both faces of the blank smooth.

Step 8

Glue and clamp the last set of bloodwood strips to the cherry blank.

Step 9

Trim the edges of the bloodwood.

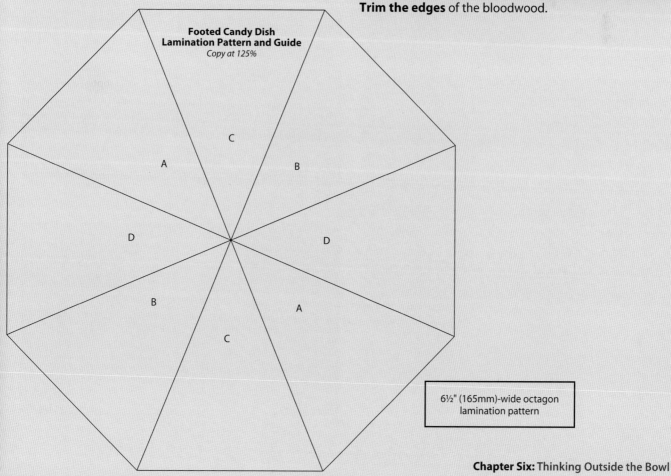

**Footed Candy Dish
Lamination Pattern and Guide**
Copy at 125%

C
A
B
D
D
B
A
C

6½" (165mm)-wide octagon lamination pattern

Making the dish

1. Mark guidelines on the blank.

2. Using the center mark and an awl, glue the cutting pattern (page 121) to the bowl blank with repositionable adhesive, aligning guidelines.

3. Cut the perimeter clockwise at a 40° angle with the saw table tilted left side down.

4. Drill a 40° entry hole and cut along the inner circle to complete the first ring.

5. Place the ring on the bowl blank, align the guidelines, and mark both sides of the ring to create the cutting lines for the second ring.

6. Cut clockwise along the outer edge of the second ring with the table tilted 38°, left side down. This cut removes the excess material that remains when a ring is cut at an angle that is much steeper than usual.

7. Drill a 38° entry hole and cut the inner edge of the second ring at a 38° angle.

8. Place the second ring on the blank, align the guidelines, and draw just the outer perimeter to form the outline for the bottom piece.

9. Cut out the bottom piece at a 45° angle, saw table left side down, cutting clockwise. This is the piece to which you will attach the pedestal base.

10. Glue up the two rings. Clamp and let dry.

11. Sand the inside smooth. Be sure to keep the lower edge round. Contour the upper edge to bring out the scallop effect. The more you sand, the more pronounced the scallops become.

12. Glue on the bottom piece. Clamp and let dry.

13. Sand the outside smooth, contouring the lower edge.

Making the pedestal base

1. Using a compass, draw a 3" (76mm) circle on the 4" (102mm) piece of cherry.

2. Cut clockwise along on the circle at a 28° angle, saw table tilted left side down.

3. Trace the outline of the smaller face of the piece you just cut on the 3" (76mm) piece of cherry.

4. With the saw table level, cut out the circle. This piece will form the neck of the pedestal base.

5. Glue both pieces together, keeping the grains aligned. Clamp and let dry.

6. Contour the pedestal using a spindle sander.

7. Glue the pedestal to the bowl. Weight down and let dry.

8. Do touch-up sanding as needed and finish as desired.

Step 5

Glue the neck and base together.

Step 7

Glue the pedestal to the bowl.

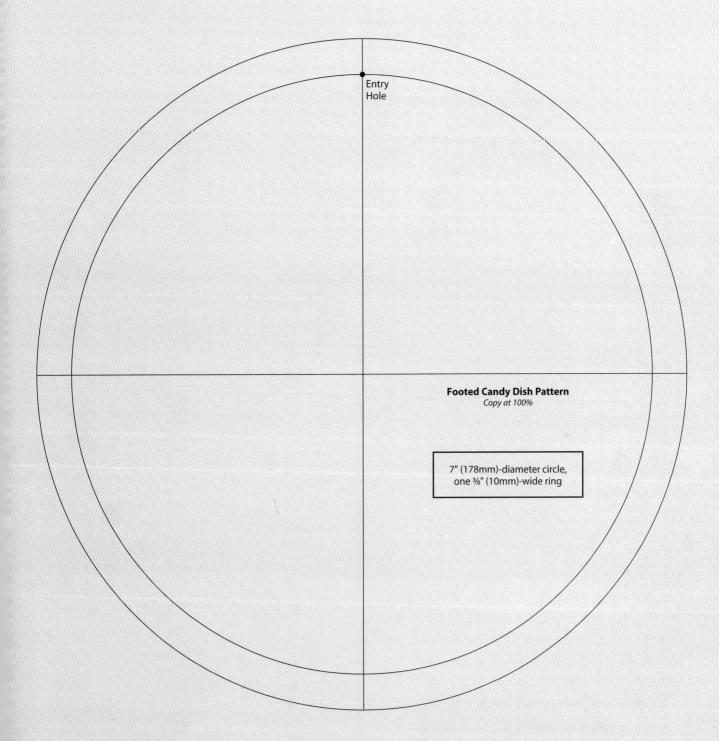

Entry
Hole

Footed Candy Dish Pattern
Copy at 100%

7" (178mm)-diameter circle,
one ⅜" (10mm)-wide ring

121

This colorful vase uses a two-step cutting process to create contour, and inserts of contrasting wood to add color and interest. While many steps are required, the construction is quite simple: two bowls joined with a center ring, topped by a matching neck assembly. The vase uses a lamination for the center ring, but a solid ring will also work, and is given as an option. Be sure to keep the grain running in the same direction for all pieces.

Materials and Tools

Wood

Body of vase:
- ❖ (2) 7½" x 7½" x ¾" (191mm x 191mm x 19mm) mahogany
- ❖ (2) 6" x 6" x ⅛" (152mm x 152mm x 3mm) purpleheart

Center ring:
- ❖ (1) 7" (178mm) round completed lamination from the Eight-Segment Bowl, page 81
- ❖ (2) 7½" x 7½" x ⅛" (191mm x 191mm x 3mm) purpleheart

Alternate center ring:
- ❖ (1) 7½" x 7½" x ½" (191mm x 191mm x 13mm) purpleheart

Neck of vase:
- ❖ (1) 4" x 4" x ¾" (102mm x 102mm x 19mm) mahogany

Top rim of vase:
- ❖ (1) 5" x 5" x ¾" (127mm x 127mm x 19mm) mahogany

Materials
- ❖ Packing tape (optional)
- ❖ Glue
- ❖ Repositionable adhesive
- ❖ Sanding discs for flexible pad sander, assorted grits 60 to 400
- ❖ Sandpaper for inflatable ball sander, assorted grits 60 to 320
- ❖ Sandpaper for hand sanding, assorted grits 220 to 400
- ❖ 0000 steel wool or 320-grit sanding sponge
- ❖ Spray shellac or Danish oil

Tools
- ❖ Scroll saw blade, size #9
- ❖ Drill bit size #54 or ¹⁄₁₆" (2mm)
- ❖ Awl
- ❖ Ruler
- ❖ Compass
- ❖ Bowl press or clamps
- ❖ 2" (51mm) flexible pad sander
- ❖ Inflatable ball sander and pump

Making the lower section of the vase body

1. Draw guidelines on one 7½" (191mm) mahogany blank and glue the vase body pattern (page 125) in place with repositionable adhesive, using the awl to align it with the guidelines.

2. Cut the outline of the first ring at a 20° angle, saw table tilted left side down, cutting clockwise.

3. Drill a 20° entry hole and complete the first ring.

4. Mark the top of the first ring and transfer the guidelines.

5. Place the first ring on the blank and mark the outline for the second ring.

6. Drill a 25° entry hole for the second ring.

7. Before cutting out the second ring, re-cut the outside of the blank at 25°, keeping the top edge the same size. This extra cut adds contour and reduces the amount of shaping needed when you sand the vase.

8. Cut the inside of the second ring at 25°.

9. Place the second ring, narrow side down, on one of the 6" (152mm) pieces of ⅛" (3mm) purpleheart and trace the inner and outer outlines. Keep the grains oriented in the same direction.

10. Drill a 25° entry hole on the inner circle of the purpleheart.

11. Cut clockwise along both circles at a 25° angle to form the third ring. Save the center piece of purpleheart to use for the neck lamination.

12. Place the purpleheart ring on the mahogany blank and use it to mark the inner and outer outlines of the fourth ring.

13. Drill a 30° entry hole on the inner ring and cut the fourth ring at 30°, saw table tilted left side down, cutting clockwise.

14. Trace only the outer perimeter of the fourth ring on the remainder of the mahogany blank.

15. Cut along the traced line at 35°, saw table left side down, cutting clockwise. This piece will be the bottom of the vase.

Making the upper section of the vase body

1. Repeat Steps 1–12 of "Making the lower section of the vase body."

2. Drill a 35° entry hole on the inner circle of the fourth ring and cut the fourth ring at 35°, saw table tilted left side down, cutting clockwise. The remaining piece of the blank will be the bottom of the neck assembly. It is left as-is to allow maximum wood for shaping in Step 3 of "Completing the vase."

Step 7

Trim the outside of the second ring at 25°, but do not cut the top edge.

Step 9

Trace the outlines of the second ring onto the purpleheart. Note the piece shown is round because it was a remainder from another project.

Assembling the lower and upper sections

1. Glue up the four rings (three mahogany and one purpleheart) for each section of the vase. Clamp and let dry.

2. Sand the inside of each ring set lightly, since it will not be seen.

3. Glue the vase bottom to the lower ring set. Clamp and let dry.

4. Sand the outside of both parts of the vase body to remove ridges. Final shaping and sanding will be done when the vase is assembled.

Another use for inserted rings

Although contrasting rings are usually inserted for decorative purposes, you can use them to replace rings that have been miscut or damaged. If you can incorporate the substitution into your design, no one will know you didn't plan it that way.

Rounded Vase with Laminated Rings

Making the center ring of the vase

1A. If using the laminated blank from the Eight Segment Bowl, glue the two 7½" x 7½" x ⅛" (191mm x 191mm x 3mm) pieces of purpleheart to the lamination, one on each face. Keep the grains of the purpleheart aligned. Clamp and let dry. Mark center. Attach the center ring pattern (page 125) with repositionable adhesive and cut a straight-sided ring 6½" (165mm) in diameter and ⅜" (10mm) wide. Save the piece left over to use in another project.

1B. If you're using a ½" (13mm) piece of purpleheart for the center of the vase, use the center ring pattern (page 125) to cut a straight-sided ring 6½" (165mm) in diameter and ⅜" (10mm) wide. Save the piece left over for another project.

2. Glue the decorative ring to the lower section of the vase. Clamp and let dry.

Making the neck assembly

1. Measure the diameter of the larger face of the piece reserved from the top ring set. This piece is the bottom of the neck assembly. It should be about 4¼" (108mm).

2. Draw a circle of the measured diameter on the 5" x 5" x ¾" (127mm x 127mm x 19mm) piece of mahogany. Do not trace the bottom of the neck assembly—if the piece is irregular, the error will be compounded. If a true circle is cut, any irregularities can be more easily corrected.

3. Cut out the circle clockwise at a 35° angle, saw table tilted left side down. This piece is the top of the neck assembly.

4. Glue the 4" x 4" x ¾" (102mm x 102mm x 19mm) piece of mahogany between the two pieces of ⅛" (3mm) purpleheart that were left over after cutting the purpleheart rings for the body of the vase. Keep the grains running in the same direction. This will be the middle of the neck assembly. Clamp and let dry.

5. Place the top piece of the neck assembly, wide side up, on the middle piece and trace the lower edge to form a circle. Mark the center of this circle.

6. Use a compass to draw a circle inside the one you just drew that will give you a ring that is about ½" (13mm) wide. You need a wide ring to allow for shaping in Step 12.

7. With the saw table level, cut along both circles, drilling an entry hole to cut out the middle. This is the completed middle piece of the neck assembly.

8. Place the top piece of the neck assembly so that the larger face is down. Center the completed middle piece on top and trace the inner circle. Repeat for the bottom piece of the neck assembly. See photo for Double Swirl Vase, Step 19, page 105.

9. For both top and bottom pieces of the neck assembly, drill a 35° angle entry hole on the circle drawn in Step 8. The hole should face the *edge*, not the center.

10. Cut out the center hole for both pieces with the table tilted at 35°, left side down, cutting *counterclockwise*. Discard the center cut-out piece. See photo for Double Swirl Vase, Step 20, page 105.

11. Glue the middle of the neck assembly between the upper and lower pieces, keeping the grains aligned. See photo for Double Swirl Vase, Step 22, page 105. Clamp and let dry.

12. Shape the neck assembly on the spindle sander and smooth the center hole. Use the inflatable ball sander to contour the upper rim. See photos for Double Swirl Vase, Steps 23 and 24, pages 105–106.

Completing the vase

1. Glue the upper part of the vase body to the lower part, keeping the grains aligned. Weight down and let dry.

2. Glue the neck assembly on top, keeping grains aligned. Place weight on top and let dry.

3. Complete the shaping and sanding.

4. Finish as desired.

Step 1

The three assemblies prior to gluing. The neck center hole has not been cut yet in this photo.

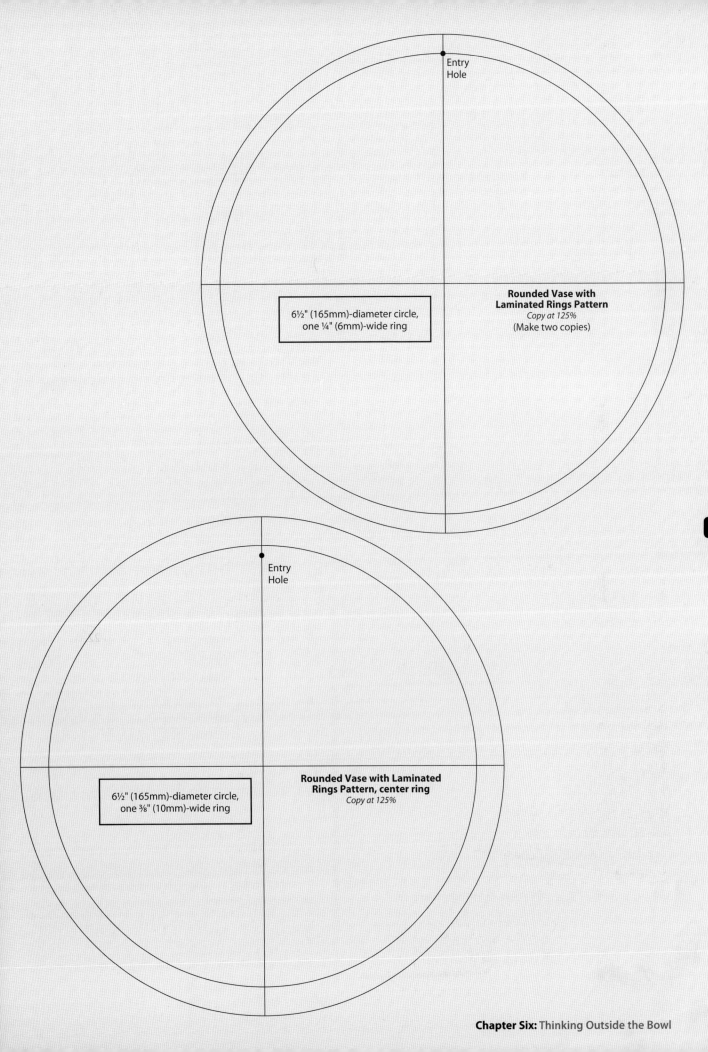

• Entry
Hole

6½" (165mm)-diameter circle,
one ¼" (6mm)-wide ring

**Rounded Vase with
Laminated Rings Pattern**
Copy at 125%
(Make two copies)

• Entry
Hole

6½" (165mm)-diameter circle,
one ⅜" (10mm)-wide ring

**Rounded Vase with Laminated
Rings Pattern, center ring**
Copy at 125%

126

This elegant vase is the wooden version of a glass one that came with a bouquet of Mother's Day flowers. It uses the same top rim as the Ripple-Edged Round Bowl, page 70, but in a smaller version. As with the other projects in this chapter, it is constructed from several sets of rings. I decided to use aspen for its ivory-like appearance, which I felt complemented the shape of the vase. I also liked the idea of ending the book with a complex project made from the same wood as the very first simple bowl, to highlight the versatility of the techniques underlying the construction of scroll saw bowls.

Materials and Tools

Wood
Ring sets 1, 2, and 3:
- (3) 6" x 6" x ¾" (152mm x 152mm x 19mm) aspen

Top ring:
- (1) 5" x 5" x ¾" (127mm x 127mm x 19mm) aspen

Neck ring:
- (1) 4" x 4" x ¾" (102mm x 102mm x 19mm) aspen

Materials
- Packing tape (optional)
- Glue
- Repositionable adhesive
- Sanding discs for flexible pad sander, assorted grits 60 to 400
- Sandpaper for inflatable ball sander, assorted grits 60 to 320
- Sandpaper for hand sanding, assorted grits 220 to 400
- 0000 steel wool or 320-grit sanding sponge
- Spray shellac

Tools
- Scroll saw blade, size #9
- Drill bit size #54 or ¹⁄₁₆" (2mm)
- Awl
- Ruler
- Bowl press or clamps
- 2" (51mm) flexible pad sander
- Inflatable ball sander and pump

Note: The vase is constructed in three sections: body, neck, and top ring, each completed before being joined together. The only component that may cause difficulty is the top ring, whose small size makes sanding quite demanding. However, because this piece uses very little wood, you can make more than one, if necessary, until you are satisfied with the results. As always, when using several different pieces of wood, it is important to keep the grain running in the same direction.

Making the body

1. Draw guidelines on one of the 6" (152mm) pieces of aspen and glue on the pattern for ring set 1 (page 130) with repositionable adhesive.

2. Cut along the outer line at a 20° angle, saw table tilted left side down, cutting clockwise.

3. Drill a 20° entry hole and complete the first ring.

4. Place the first ring on the bowl blank, mark the top, and transfer guidelines. Mark the outline for the second ring.

5. Drill a 20° entry hole.

6. Cut out and mark the second ring.

7. Cut out and mark the third ring in the same manner.

8. Glue up the three rings, clamp, and let dry.

9. Sand inside lightly, since it will not be seen.

10. Glue on the bottom piece. Clamp and let dry. Sand the outside smooth, keeping the top edge as wide as possible.

11. Glue the pattern for the center ring (page 130) to a second 6" (152mm) piece of aspen with repositionable adhesive.

12. With the saw table level, cut along the outer circle.

13. Drill a straight entry hole just inside the inner ring and cut out the ring. Save the center piece to use for one of the neck rings.

14. Draw guidelines on the third 6" (152mm) piece of aspen and glue on the pattern for ring set 2 (page 130) with repositionable adhesive.

15. Cut along the outer circle with the saw table set at 34°, left side down, cutting clockwise.

16. Drill a 34° entry hole on the inner circle and complete the ring, cutting clockwise. You will have one ring and a remaining piece.

17. Tilt the saw table to 45°, left side down. Using the top edge as a guide, cut clockwise around the perimeter of the remaining piece, wider side up. The top edge should remain the same size.

18. Glue this piece to the ring. Clamp and let dry.

19. Sand inside lightly.

Step 8

Glue up the three rings of set 1.

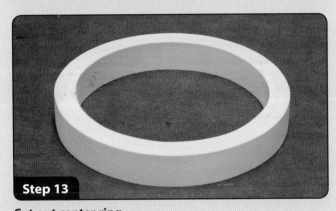

Step 13

Cut out center ring.

Step 18

Glue-up ring set 2.

127

Making the rippled top ring

1. Glue the pattern for the top ring (page 131) to the 5" (127mm) piece of aspen with repositionable adhesive.

2. Cut along the outer circle of the ring at a 35° angle, saw table tilted left side down, cutting clockwise.

3. Drill a 25° entry hole just inside the inner circle and cut along the inner circle at a 25° angle, saw table left side down, cutting clockwise. The bottom diameter of the ring should be about 3¾" (95mm).

4. Glue the ripple edge pattern (page 131) to the top of the ring with repositionable adhesive.

5. Tilt the saw table to 40°, left side down, and cut along the inner line, cutting clockwise. Avoid cutting into the lower edge.

6. Tilt the table to 15°, left side down, and cut along the outer line, cutting clockwise.

7. Sand the inside and outside of the rippled ring, using an inflatable ball sander. You will complete the sanding later.

Step 4

Glue the ripple edge pattern to the top ring.

Steps 5 & 6

Cut the inner edge at 40° and the outer edge at 15°.

Step 7

Sand the top ring.

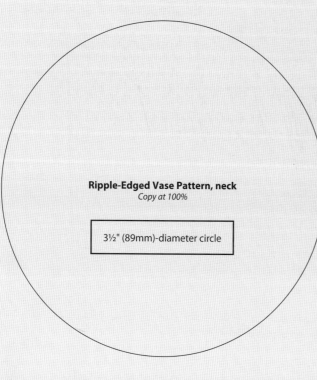

Ripple-Edged Vase Pattern, neck
Copy at 100%

3½" (89mm)-diameter circle

128

Wooden Bowls from the Scroll Saw

Making the neck

1. Place the neck pattern (page 128) on the piece of aspen saved from cutting ring 2 in Step 13 of Making the body. This will become one of the neck rings.

2. Cut out the circle at a 10° angle, saw table tilted left side down, cutting clockwise. Keep this piece wide side up and center the rippled top ring on top, keeping grains of both pieces aligned. It should overhang the neck slightly, and will be sanded down later.

3. Trace the inner circle of the rippled ring onto the neck.

4. Drill a slightly angled entry hole just inside the circle and cut clockwise along the circle at 10°, saw table tilted left side down.

5. Place this ring, wide side up, on the 4" (102mm) piece of aspen, making sure to align the grains. Trace the inner and outer circles. Cut clockwise along these lines at 10°, saw table tilted left side down. This is the other neck ring.

6. Glue the two rings together, wide sides up, keeping the grains aligned. Clamp and let dry.

7. Sand the inside and outside smooth.

Assembling the vase

1. Invert ring set 2 so that the solid piece is on top.

2. Center the glued-up neck pieces, wide side up, on the solid piece of ring set 2, aligning grains. Trace the inside. This will form the opening of the vase. It should be about 2⅛" (54mm) in diameter.

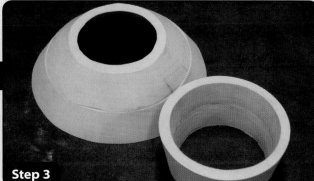

Step 3

Cut the vase opening.

3. Drill an entry hole at a 25° angle, facing the *outside* of the piece, on the circle you just traced. Cut along the circle at a 25° angle, saw table tilted left side down, cutting *counterclockwise*. You may need to cut a smaller circle first, with the table level, to allow clearance for the blade clamp.

4. Glue the rippled top ring to the wide face of the neck rings. Weight down and let dry. This forms the top assembly of the vase.

5. Finish shaping and smoothing the top assembly using the flexible pad and inflatable ball sanders. Round the lower edge of the rippled top ring where it meets the neck.

Step 6

Glue center ring to ring set 2.

6. Glue center ring to ring set 2 (inverted set with hole). Clamp and let dry. Lightly sand the inside.

7. Glue this assembly to ring set 1 (straight set of glued-up rings and base). This completes the body of the vase. Weight down and let dry.

8. Lightly trace the outline of the top assembly on the vase body. Shape and sand the vase body, keeping the area inside the outline flat for gluing.

9. Glue the top assembly to the vase body. Weight down and let dry.

10. Do touch-up sanding as needed.

Step 7

Glue ring set 2 to ring set 1.

11. Finish with several coats of shellac, sanding between coats.

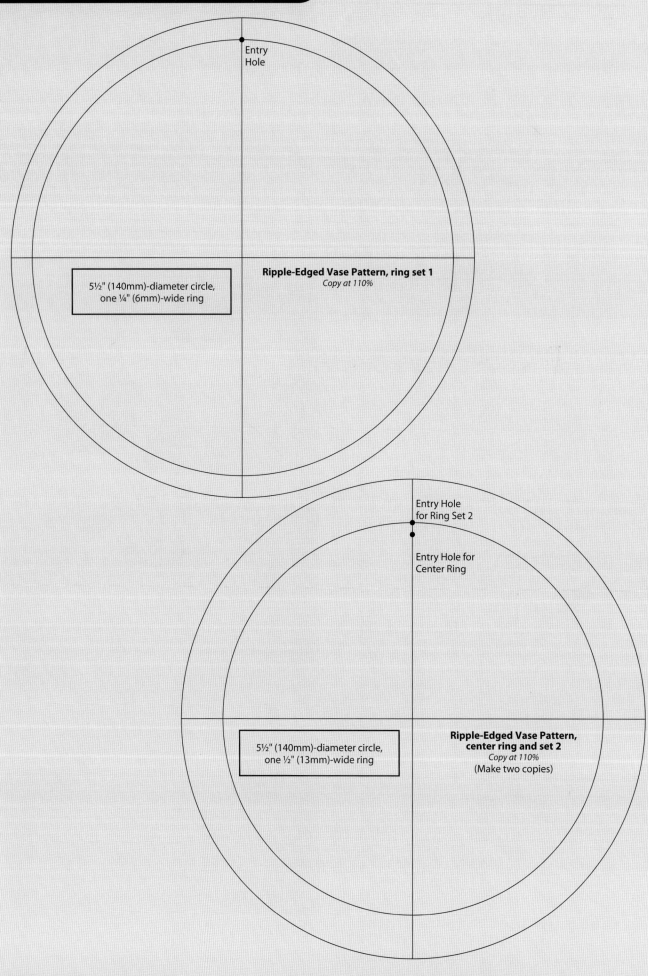

Entry
Hole

Ripple-Edged Vase Pattern, ring set 1
Copy at 110%

5½" (140mm)-diameter circle,
one ¼" (6mm)-wide ring

Entry Hole
for Ring Set 2

Entry Hole for
Center Ring

**Ripple-Edged Vase Pattern,
center ring and set 2**
Copy at 110%
(Make two copies)

5½" (140mm)-diameter circle,
one ½" (13mm)-wide ring

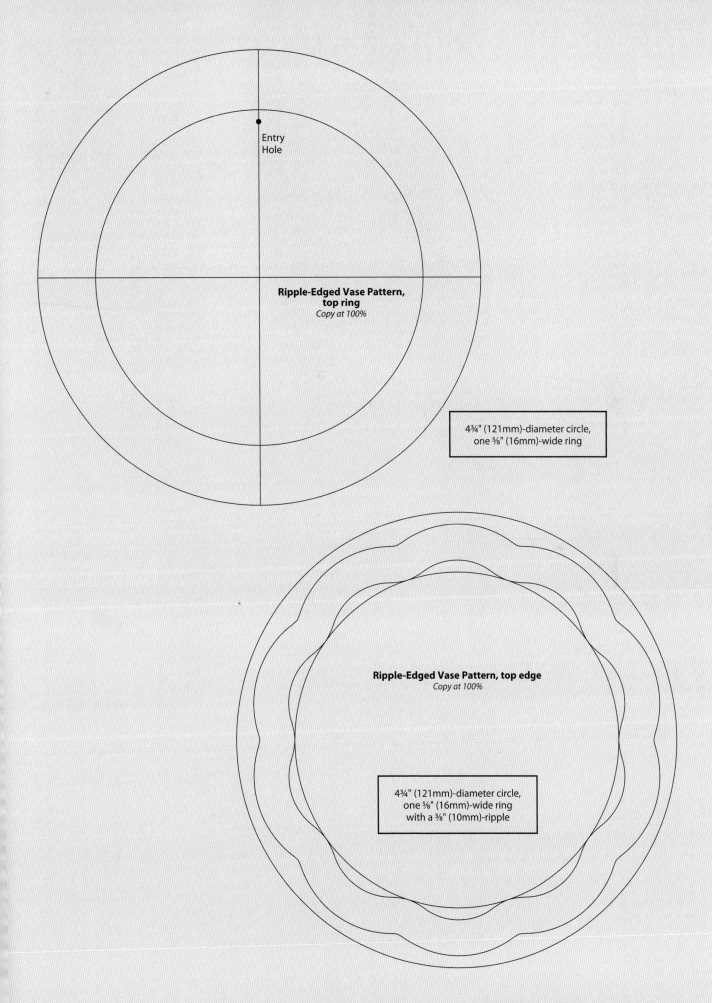

Entry
Hole

**Ripple-Edged Vase Pattern,
top ring**
Copy at 100%

4¾" (121mm)-diameter circle,
one ⅝" (16mm)-wide ring

Ripple-Edged Vase Pattern, top edge
Copy at 100%

4¾" (121mm)-diameter circle,
one ⅝" (16mm)-wide ring
with a ⅜" (10mm)-ripple

131

Appendix: Creating Patterns

Did you ever have to buy wood for a project because what you had on hand was just a little too short, narrow, thick, or thin? Are you accumulating wonderful pieces of wood to use "one day"? By making your own patterns, or by adapting those from this book, you can use wood you already own, wood reclaimed from used furniture, or other people's castoffs. Here are some considerations to keep in mind as you move from my ideas to your own.

Use the ideas in this book to inspire your own designs.

Patterns

Pattern making for bowls is quite straightforward, especially if you use the ring method, which requires drawing only an outline and one ring. All the patterns for this book (before being redrawn for publication) were made with very low-tech equipment: ¼" (6mm) graph paper, ruler, compass, protractor, French curves, cookie cutters, and a good eraser. If you have access to software that automates the process, so much the better, but it certainly isn't necessary.

Shapes and Sizes

When planning your bowl, keep in mind that contours become smaller with each successive ring. Be sure your bowl is sized so you can cut and sand the smallest ring. If your pattern is very intricate or the wood is hard to cut, try using fewer rings, or create wider curves and corners. Sometimes a simple circle is sufficient when a piece of wood is especially interesting.

Laminations

Laminations challenge your creativity and let you take your bowl to another level. They also use up wood left over from other projects. Here are a few tips to help you get the most from your laminations.

Color

To get a good idea of how your wood combinations will look when finished, wet the pieces of wood with mineral spirits or make a test application on scraps of wood with the finish you plan to use.

Be careful when sanding strongly colored wood like padauk, the dust of which can migrate into the pores of adjacent pieces. Try to sand from light to dark, when possible.

Try using a different color combination with the same lamination pattern. If you change ring width and cutting angle as well, you'll never know it was the same bowl.

Stripes and swags

Laminated strips that run through the center of the pattern (radial) will remain straight when cut and stacked. Laminated strips that go across the rings (tangential) will form swags. I did not include instructions in the book for the multicolor bowl shown above because I found that I could not align the swags precisely enough to prevent "jaggies." However, it is a clear example of how radial and tangential strips behave.

When tangential strips, seen in the back of this bowl, are used in a lamination design, swags are formed.

Ring Basics

No matter how simple or elaborate, a bowl is only as good as the rings it uses. These hints are good to keep in mind when you plan your bowls.

Entry holes

Always put entry holes in locations that are easy to sand, such as wide curves. Try not to have two entry holes back-to-back since that reduces the amount of wood available for sanding and shaping. This is most important for ¼" wide rings—wider rings are more forgiving.

Ring width

For any given wood thickness, narrower rings can take a smaller cutting angle than wider ones. This lets you cut bowls with more vertical sides. Wider rings are useful when you are working with wood that is dense or hard to control since there is more leeway for corrective shaping and sanding. Even wide rings can produce thin-sided bowls with enough aggressive sanding—see photo below.

This aspen bowl used rings that were ½" (13mm) wide, then sanded severely.

Angles—The Final Word

For every combination of ring width and wood thickness there is a cutting angle that will result in rings that are nearly perfectly aligned. This angle is actually the smallest angle that will produce concentric rings from a single piece of wood. I call it the minimum cutting angle. If a smaller angle is used, the remaining piece of wood cannot be used for the next ring. If, however, a larger angle is used, the outer edge of the next ring can be trimmed, as is done when making bowls with curved sides.

The chart in Chapter One, page 13, gives minimum cutting angles for typical combinations of wood thickness and ring width. However, since not all wood is of standard thickness, it's useful to be able to determine the minimum cutting angle for any piece of wood. This angle is actually the amount that the saw table is moved from its normally level position, and is read on the scale under the saw table.

To find this angle, divide the ring width by the wood thickness and find the angle on the Cutting Angle Chart (below) that corresponds to your

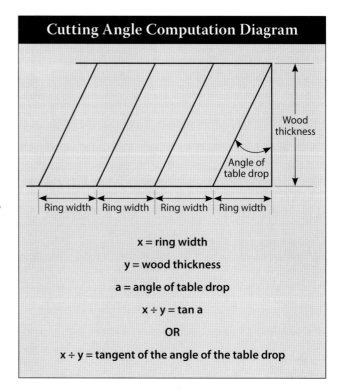

Cutting Angle Computation Diagram

x = ring width

y = wood thickness

a = angle of table drop

x ÷ y = tan a

OR

x ÷ y = tangent of the angle of the table drop

answer. For example, if your ring width is ⅜" (10mm) and your wood is ¾" (19mm) thick, divide ⅜" by ¾" (10mm by 19mm). Your answer will be .5. If you look at the cutting angle chart, you'll see that the closest number is .5095, which corresponds to a cutting angle of 27°. I like to increase the angle by one degree to provide an extra safety margin. This gives you a cutting angle of 28°. Use the same procedure for any thickness of wood and any ring width.

The cutting angle chart is really a tangent chart. You're actually computing the tangent of the cutting angle, which shows that you never know when your high school trigonometry will come in handy! See the Cutting Angle Computation Diagram (above) for an illustration of what you're computing, or just use the formula if you prefer. In either case, you'll be well equipped to figure out how to cut most any bowl successfully.

Cutting Angle Chart

Cutting Angle	Ring width ÷ wood thickness	Cutting Angle	Ring width ÷ wood thickness
15	0.2679	30	0.5773
16	0.2867	31	0.6008
17	0.3057	32	0.6248
18	0.3249	33	0.6493
19	0.3443	34	0.6744
20	0.3639	35	0.7001
21	0.3838	36	0.7265
22	0.4040	37	0.7535
23	0.4244	38	0.7812
24	0.4452	39	0.8097
25	0.4663	40	0.8390
26	0.4877	41	0.8692
27	0.5095	42	0.9003
28	0.5317	43	0.9324
29	0.5543	44	0.9656
		45	1.0000

Index

A

alignment jig, 82
angle guide, 14
angles, 13, 25, 136. *See also* multiple-angle bowls
aspen wood, 10
awl, using, 12

B

basic stacked bowls, 20–39
  about: overview of, 20–21
  Basic Bowl: A Step-by-Step Guide, 22–29
  Eight-Petal Bowl, 30–31
  Rounded-Square Bowl, 32–33
  Scrolled-Top Bowl, 36–39
  Wavy Bowl, 34–35
Basket-Weave Bowl, 46–48
beveling, 72, 111, 113, 114, 116
blade, tensioning, 13
bowl press, 16–17

C

cedar wood, 10
Center Lamination Bowl, 94–95
cherry wood, 11
color bleeding, 11
contouring bowls, 28–29. *See also* sanding and sanders
creating patterns, 132–34
Crisscross Bowl: A Step-by-Step Guide, 62–67
cutting
  angle guide for, 14
  angles, 13, 25, 136
  blade tensioning for, 13
  direction, table tilt and, 13
  drilling entry holes for, 14, 24, 133
  outline, 23
  petal edge, 73
  rings, 12, 38
  waste removal cuts, 69
  See also beveling

D

Danish oil, applying, 19
Double-Swag Bowl: A Step-by-Step Guide, 42–45
Double-Swirl Vase: A Step-by-Step Guide, 100–106
drilling entry holes, 14, 24, 133

E

Eight-Petal Bowl, 30–31
Eight-Segment Bowl: A Step-by-Step Guide, 80–85
enlarging patterns, 13
entry holes, 14, 24, 133

F

finish, selecting and applying, 19
Five-Petal Bowl, 96–97
Flared Five-Lobed Bowl, 68–69
Footed Candy Dish, 118–21
Four-Petal Curved Bowl, 74–75

G

Ginger Jar, 107–12
Gingham Bowl, 52–53
gluing and glues, 15–17
  bowl press for, 16–17
  choosing correct glue, 15
  gluing on diagonal, 63
  jig for, 82
  process, 15. *See also* step-by-step guides
  types of glues, 15
guidelines, 12, 23, 43

H

Heart-Shaped Bowl, 76–77

J

jars. *See* outside-the-bowl patterns

L

laminated wood bowls, 40–59
  about: color, strips and swags, 133; creating patterns, 133; overview of, 40–41; wood for, 10, 11
  Basket-Weave Bowl, 46–48
  Double-Swag Bowl: A Step-by-Step Guide, 42–45
  Gingham Bowl, 52–53
  Plaid Bowl, 49–51
  Triple-Swirl Bowl, 57–59
  Windowpane Bowl, 54–56
  See also Crisscross Bowl: A Step-by-Step Guide; outside-the-bowl patterns; thin wood bowls

M

mahogany wood, 11
maple wood, 11
marking bowls. *See* guidelines
Multi-Colored Jar, 113–17
Multi-Colored Twenty Segment Bowl, 86–89
multiple-angle bowls, 60–77
  about: overview of, 60–61
  Crisscross Bowl: A Step-by-Step Guide, 62–67
  Flared Five-Lobed Bowl, 68–69
  Four-Petal Curved Bowl, 74–75
  Heart-Shaped Bowl, 76–77
  Ripple-Edged Round Bowl, 70–73

O

oak wood, 11
outside-the-bowl patterns, 98–131
  about: overview of, 98–99
  Double-Swirl Vase: A Step-by-Step Guide, 100–106
  Footed Candy Dish, 118–21
  Ginger Jar, 107–12
  Multi-Colored Jar, 113–17
  Ripple-Edged Vase, 126–31
  Rounded Vase with Laminated Rings, 122–25
Oval Bowl, 92–93

P

padauk, working with, 48, 133
patterns
  aligning, 23
  creating, 132–34
  enlarging, 13
  guidelines, 12, 23, 43
Plaid Bowl, 49–51
poplar wood, 10
PVA glues, 15

R

rings
  cutting, 12, 38
  width of, creating patterns and, 133
Ripple-Edged Round Bowl, 70–73
Ripple-Edged Vase, 126–31
Rounded Vase with Laminated Rings, 122–25
Rounded-Square Bowl, 32–33

S

sanding and sanders, 18, 23
Scrolled-Top Bowl, 36–39
Seven-Lobe Ripple-Edged Bowl, 90–91
shellac, applying, 19
step-by-step guides
  Basic Bowl, 22–29
  Crisscross Bowl (multiple-angle bowl), 62–67
  Double-Swag Bowl (laminated), 42–45
  Double-Swirl Vase, 100–106
  Eight-Segment Bowl (thin bowl), 80–85

T

taping, 23
thin wood bowls, 78–97
  about: overview of, 78–79
  Center Lamination Bowl, 94–95
  Eight-Segment Bowl: A Step-by-Step Guide, 80–85
  Five-Petal Bowl, 96–97
  Multi-Colored Twenty Segment Bowl, 86–89
  Oval Bowl, 92–93
  Seven-Lobe Ripple-Edged Bowl, 90–91
Triple-Swirl Bowl, 57–59

U

urea-formaldehyde glue, 15

V

vases. *See* outside-the-bowl patterns

W

walnut wood, 11
waste removal cuts, 69
Wavy Bowl, 34–35
Windowpane Bowl, 54–56
wood
  choosing, 10–11
  for lamination, 10, 11
  recycled, 11
  See also **specific species of wood**

More Great Books from Fox Chapel Publishing

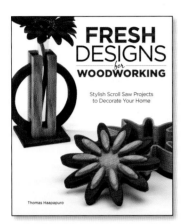

Fresh Designs for Woodworking
ISBN 978-1-56523-537-3 **$19.99**

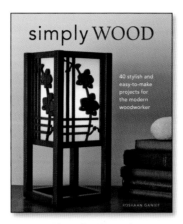

Simply Wood
ISBN 978-1-56523-440-6 **$19.95**

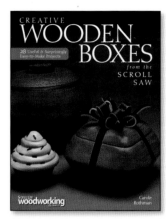

**Creative Wooden Boxes
from the Scroll Saw**
ISBN 978-1-56523-541-0 **$24.95**

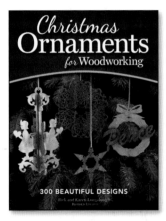

**Christmas Ornaments for
Woodworking, Revised Edition**
ISBN 978-1-56523-788-9 **$16.99**

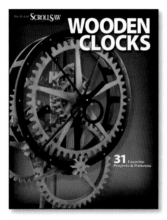

Wooden Clocks
ISBN 978-1-56523-427-7 **$24.95**

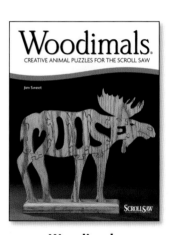

Woodimals
ISBN 978-1-56523-748-3 **$16.99**

In addition to being a leading source of woodworking books and DVDs, Fox Chapel also publishes two premiere magazines. Released quarterly, each delivers premium projects, expert tips and techniques from today's finest woodworking artists, and in-depth information about the latest tools, equipment, and materials.

Subscribe Today!
Woodcarving Illustrated: **888-506-6630**
Scroll Saw Woodworking & Crafts: **888-840-8590**
www.FoxChapelPublishing.com